Word & Image
Art, Books
and Design

FROM THE NATIONAL ART LIBRARY

Word & Image
Art, Books
and Design

FROM THE NATIONAL ART LIBRARY

Edited by Rowan Watson,
Elizabeth James and Julius Bryant

V&A Publishing

First published by V&A Publishing, 2015

V&A Publishing
Victoria and Albert Museum
South Kensington
London SW7 2RL
www.vandapublishing.com

ISBN: 978 1 85177 808 9
Library of Congress Catalog Control Number 2014932331

10 9 8 7 6 5 4 3 2 1
2018 2017 2016 2015

A catalogue record for this book is available from the British Library.

Designed by Heather Bowen
Copy-edited by Delia Gaze
Index by Hilary Bird
New V&A photography by Paul Robins, V&A Photographic Studio

Jacket illustration: see pl.133
Frontispiece: detail of fig.34
p.6: Folios from the Codex Forster, a series of five notebooks compiled by Leonardo da Vinci
when in Florence and Milan between c.1487 and 1505. The notebooks were bound into three
volumes in the early seventeenth century and given to John Forster in c.1868.
p.8: From Louis Renard, *Poissons, écrevisses, et crabes* (1754); see pl.5
p.10: The entrance to the National Art Library
p.26: From Grüner, *Fresco Decorations* (1844); see pl.20
p.44: Book altered with photomontage; see pl.140
p.173: The main Reading Room of the National Art Library

Printed in China

V&A Publishing

Supporting the world's leading
museum of art and design,
the Victoria and Albert
Museum, London

Contents

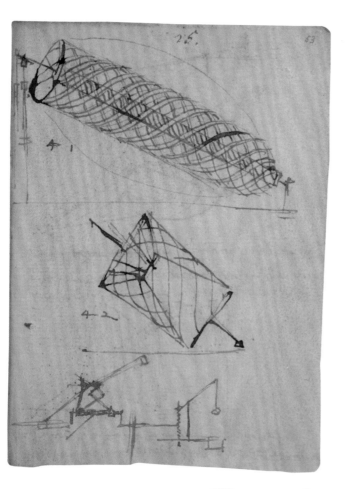

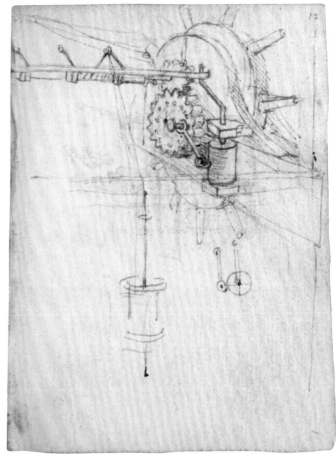

Director's Foreword

Among the many qualities and resources that make the Victoria and Albert Museum so different from other national museums in London, the National Art Library stands out. Situated at the heart of the Museum, overlooking the beautiful courtyard garden, the Library is one of the most inspiring and memorable places to work. Across the reflecting pool below, it faces the Museum's original front entrance, which leads into the first purpose-built museum restaurant, with the lecture theatre above. Research and learning were key ingredients of the new kind of museum that the V&A presented when it opened in South Kensington in 1857. Taking a popular approach, the Museum sought to attract visitors from all walks of life, from craftsmen to collectors, from designers to dedicated scholars. The Library has always been open to all, and today it supports the creative industries, international scholarship and London's world-leading position in the art and antiques trade.

This publication accompanies the first international touring exhibition of treasures from the National Art Library. The selection – organized into seven sections that show distinctive facets of the unique collections – illustrates how the library has been a source of inspiration and understanding from its earliest days in the Government School of Design (later the Royal College of Art). The Museum was founded at a time of intense debate about the place and nature of art and design in an industrialized environment, and that debate is no less intense today. The Library continues to provide material that fuels and informs such discussion, making it available to an increasingly diverse range of readers.

This publication would not have been possible without the generous support of Dr Susan Weber, together with support from the Iris Foundation. I congratulate the staff of the Word and Image Department on their enterprise and industry and look forward to future showings drawn from the rich holdings of the largest and oldest collections department in the V&A.

MARTIN ROTH
Director, Victoria And Albert Museum

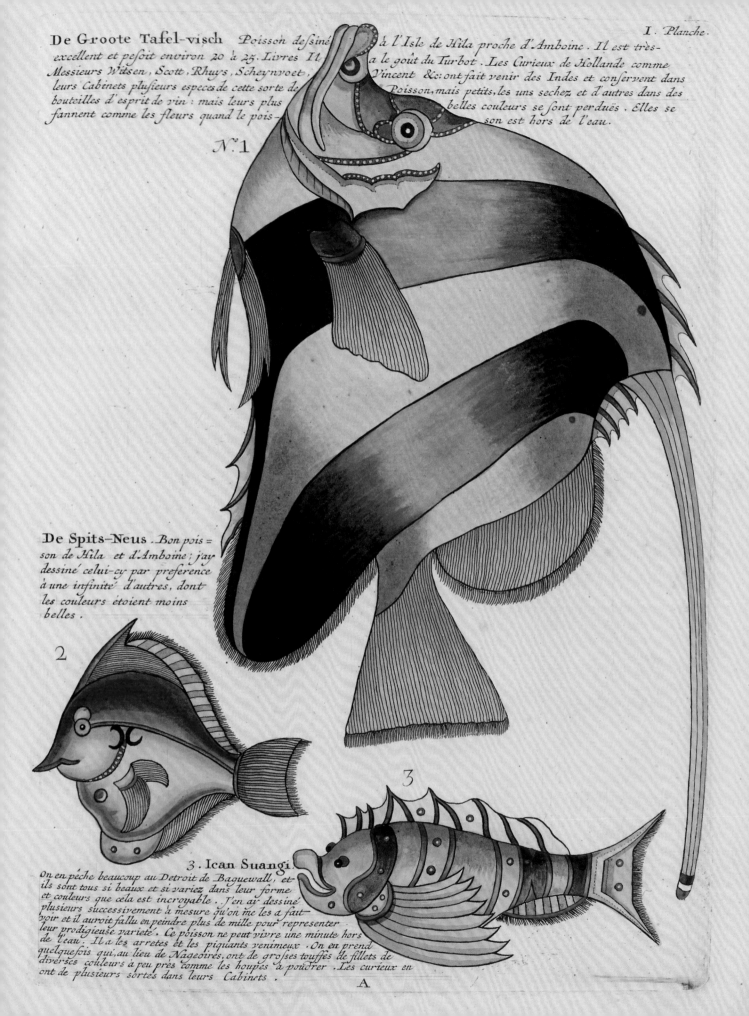

De Groote Tafel-visch Poisson dessiné à l'Isle de Hila proche d'Amboine. Il est très-
excellent et pesoit environ 20 à 25. Livres Il, a le goût du Turbot. Les Curieux de Hollande comme
Messieurs Witsen, Scott, Rhuys, Scheynvoet, Vincent &c: ont fait venir des Indes et conservent dans
leurs Cabinets plusieurs especes de cette sorte de Poisson, mais petits, les uns sechez et d'autres dans des
bouteilles d'esprit de vin : mais leurs plus belles couleurs se sont perduës. Elles se
fannent comme les fleurs quand le pois- son est hors de l'eau.

N.º 1.

De Spits-Neus. Bon pois =
son de Hila et d'Amboine ; j'ay
dessiné celui-cy par preference
à une infinité d'autres, dont
les couleurs étoient moins
belles.

2

3

3. Ican Suangi.

On en pêche beaucoup au Detroit de Baguewall, et
ils sont tous si beaux et si variez dans leur forme
et couleurs que cela est incroyable. J'en ai dessiné
plusieurs successivement à mesure qu'on me les a fait
voir et il auroit fallu en peindre plus de mille pour representer
leur prodigieuse varieté. Ce poisson ne peut vivre une minute hors
de l'eau. Il a les arretes et les piquants venimeux. On en prend
quelquefois qui, au lieu de Nageoires, ont de grosses touffes de fillets de
diverses couleurs à peu près comme les houpes à poudrer. Les curieux en
ont de plusieurs sortes dans leurs Cabinets.

A

A Reader's Foreword

I am a huge evangelist for the National Art Library. Much of the research for *The Hare with Amber Eyes* was done sitting at a desk in the library, overlooking the courtyard of the V&A. I grew to love both the atmosphere of the place and the richness and depth of its holdings.

The library is one of the pillars on which the Museum stands and is the starting place for understanding how the arts are refracted into words and how words can make art happen. The library allows passionate scholarship to flourish. In my time working there it has been a joy to observe students working alongside independent researchers and museum curators. The National Art Library stands as an important reflection of what the V&A is really about.

EDMUND DE WAAL

'Word and Image': The Evolution of the Victoria and Albert Museum's Library

JULIUS BRYANT

'Word and Image' is a simple phrase, but one that resonates. Like 'Art and Design', it identifies not only two rich fields but also the dynamic intersection where they meet. In academic circles 'Word and Image' denotes the study of the interrelationship of verbal and visual languages. Themes range from the Renaissance debate comparing the processes and appreciation of poetry, painting, sculpture and other analogous arts (*ut pictura poesis*) to the ability of language to put an image into words (*ekphrasis*).[1] From earliest times and ages, when spoken words are expressed as pictures or text, they become a visual art of communication.

In 2003 the Victoria and Albert Museum (V&A) launched a new department, Word and Image, formed to unite the National Art Library (NAL) with Prints, Drawings and Paintings. It brings together the collections of graphic arts and publications along with their librarians, archivists, curators and three sets of study rooms. The Word and Image Department is now responsible for nine national collections; these range from designs (especially for architecture) to the art of photography, and from commercial graphics (including posters) to British watercolours and drawings.[2] This publication celebrates the collections devoted to the art and design of books and publishing. They explore the challenge of capturing and communicating visual and verbal ideas, both to inform and to inspire.

This brief introduction provides a concise history of the National Art Library in terms of its evolving ambitions, shifting priorities and driving personalities. The following two chapters introduce the growth of its collections and the engagement with modern and living artists through the arts of the book. The seven catalogue sections comprise a selection from the wide range of the collections that reflects the V&A's impact on art education, graphic design, advertising, publishing and book art.

The Museums and Libraries Movement

In the second half of the nineteenth century, following the Industrial Revolution in the western world, the founding of new museums and libraries spread at a phenomenal rate. Government policies and the benevolence of the newly wealthy led efforts to spread learning through new institutions. This social investment came partly in an attempt to help quell the dissatisfaction that had led to Europe being torn apart by the political revolutions of 1848–9. But it was also in order to raise public standards of taste, as the Industrial Revolution had led to mass-produced goods of poor quality. In Britain, the Public Libraries Act (1850) enabled local authorities in larger towns and cities to tax citizens to pay for free public libraries. The public library movement spread with the promotion of adult education through working men's colleges.[3] In the USA, 2,240 new libraries opened between 1850 and 1875.[4] Between 1897 and his death in 1919 the Pittsburgh steel magnate from Scotland, Andrew Carnegie, gave grants for 2,811 free public libraries, of which 1,946 were in the USA and 660 in the UK and the rest of the English-speaking world.[5]

Britain led the world through the Industrial Revolution but followed Germany in recognizing that mass production raised the necessity of design reform.[6] As a legacy of the Great Exhibition, the first 'World's Fair' of manufactured goods, held in London in 1851, a new kind of museum with a mission was founded in South Kensington. Powered by its own art school and a library alongside, it became a prototype for similar

fig.1. The National Art Library,
as seen from the V&A's garden.
The 17-bay range, completed
in 1884, was built by General
Henry Scott (1822–1883), using
designs by Captain Francis Fowke
(1823–1865).

museums across the world. The National Art Library is the best known – and still a world leader – of this kind of specialist art museum library. Museums founded following the V&A's example include the K.K. Österreichisches Museum für Kunst und Industrie (today the 'MAK') in Vienna (founded 1864), the Metropolitan Museum of Art in New York (1870), the Art Institute of Chicago (1882) and the Museum of Decorative Arts in Prague (1885, home today to the largest art library in the Czech Republic).[7]

Histories of museums frequently trace their origins to cabinets of curiosities and the *Kunstkammer*.[8] In Britain, for example, the Ashmolean Museum in Oxford (founded 1679) is always cited as the oldest museum, in the absence of the kind of cathedral treasuries and princely cabinets found in the older cities of continental Europe. Britain lacks such collections due to its Reformation (1529–36) and Civil War (1642–8). The deepest roots of museums, however, are in libraries, specifically the library of the Ptolemies in Alexandria, part of a group of buildings dating from the fourth century BC called the *museion*.[9]

The importance of this distinction is to stress the fundamental role of museums, not only in providing visual delight and spiritual uplift as in cabinets and treasuries, but also in offering ways to structure knowledge of the material world and hence systems of thought. The basic need to shelve and retrieve books covering a myriad of subjects demands a rational process of categorization. The seemingly simple acts of indexing and storage before research can commence both reflect and influence the definition of academic disciplines in universities and curatorial departments in museums. In the Internet age, when individuals expect to access the world of knowledge through their laptop computer, it is easy to forget that most of the places where we look to find books have been chosen by scholars and librarians. For the history of art, encompassing the applied arts, design history and material culture, the National Art Library at the V&A has had a formative role in creating and defining its expanding frontiers.[10]

Visitors to the V&A often stand amazed at the Library's entrance, as readers squeeze by them at the glass doors. The

reading rooms are the Museum's most intact furnished historic
interiors. They are also one of the best-loved places in the
world in which to study the history of art and design. Whether
working in the reading rooms today, or just gazing across to
the original entrance pavilion, readers both young and old find
inspiration in this unique setting. The suite of three purpose-
built rooms forms one side of the courtyard garden, right
at the heart of the Museum. In early architectural proposals
to expand the V&A the library was even more prominent,
for it stood right at the front entrance. As the Museum's
entrance moved south, so a grand staircase was planned for the
new main hall, to provide direct access to the library's central
reading room. This location would have left visitors in no
doubt that the Museum was not only for enjoyment but also
to provide knowledge and inspiration. In the same way, the
V&A's first permanent entrance (now facing into the garden)
has the lecture theatre directly overhead, above the inscription
'Better it is to get wisdom than Gold'.

The National Art Library at the V&A has a threefold role.
First, there is its most obvious service, to readers, who range
from general visitors to professors of art history and artists.
Second, the Library underpins the expertise of the Museum's
curators and other staff and volunteers in supporting their
research on all the collections. Third, the Library serves as

a full curatorial department, responsible for covering art
and design in publishing. The historical origins of these
roles are complex. The Museum is traditionally described as
part of the legacy of the Great Exhibition of 1851, as one of
several museums and university colleges established close
to the original site of the 'Crystal Palace', the first of many
international cultural quarters founded in the footprints
of great World's Fairs. The origins of the Museum, however,
can be traced back further.

In 1835 the House of Commons Select Committee on
Arts and Manufactures reported on the reasons why many
of Britain's commercial products failed to compete against
foreign imports and failed to find markets abroad. The
Committee sought 'the best means of extending knowledge
of the arts and the principles of design among the people
(especially the manufacturing population of the country)'.[11]
The first expert witness summoned was Dr Gustav Friedrich
Waagen, director of the Royal Museum in Berlin. He described
Prussia's school of industrial arts, the Kunstgewerbeschule,
founded in Berlin in 1821, which had drawing classes,
workshops and a collection that included 'the newest
discoveries in Europe, and particularly England', plaster casts
of sculpture and ornamental decoration, and a library.[12] The
Committee recommended the founding of a nationwide
network of Schools of Design, together with public galleries,
museums and libraries to develop consumer taste. This art
education movement was part of the broader phenomenon
that accelerated the provision of libraries, schools and
universities around the world in the second half of the
nineteenth century.

The School of Design's first London home opened in
Somerset House in 1837 in palatial top-floor rooms recently
vacated by the Royal Academy.[13] For a school of design,
established to train a different kind of artist from those
produced by the Royal Academy Schools, the first library had
a wide range of literature. The School sought not only to help
train craftsmen in practical skills but also to develop their
'critical knowledge of art'.[14]

According to a report by the School's librarian, Walter R. Deverell (d.1853),[15] in 1846 its 850 books covered 'treatises on the history, theoretic principles and practice of Fine Art in general, elementary manuals on Architecture, Practical Geometry, Optics, Perspective, Anatomy and every obtainable work on the application of art to manufacture and decoration'. The Library also provided books 'conducive to mental elevation and refinement such as critical essays on Beauty, Taste and Imagination; the works of some of the great descriptive Poets . . . and, for the excitement of emulation, Biographies of Artists and others, who by genius and perseverance have acquired honourable distinction'.[16]

Following the Great Exhibition, the School of Design was relaunched as part of a new Government-funded Department of Practical Art, based initially in Marlborough House, a royal residence next to St James's Palace, lent for the purpose by Prince Albert. Here in 1852 the Art Library first opened alongside the School, the new Museum of Ornamental Art (comprising the School's teaching collections and exemplary manufactured objects purchased from the Great Exhibition) and the National Gallery's galleries of British paintings. The Art Library occupied three rooms at Marlborough House and was open from 10am to 9pm every day except Sundays (evening opening was not provided on Saturdays). As the Library faced a wider audience, so the practice of removing pages of illustrations from books for pupils to copy ceased.[17]

Early acquisitions included expensive illustrated books such as Owen Jones's *Alhambra* (1842, 1845) and *Grammar of Ornament* (1856), Leo von Klenze's *Koenigsbau* (1842) and Ludwig Grüner's *Fresco Decorations and Stuccoes of Churches and Palaces of Italy* (1844).[18] Many were purchased for the Library by Ludwig Grüner (Prince Albert's architect) on buying trips on the Continent. The School also collected prints, paintings, photographs and plaster casts to provide a visual history of art and design.

In 1857, when Prince Albert reclaimed Marlborough House for the Prince of Wales, the combined institution moved to its present site in South Kensington. The School of Design evolved into the National Art Training School, today the Royal College of Art, which occupied studios in the Museum until 1991; the College retains close links with the V&A through a joint postgraduate programme.

The 'Art Manufactures Library'
Henry Cole (1808–1882) is usually described as the first, founding director of the V&A, but as head of the new Department of Practical Art he also had nationwide responsibilities for the reformation of art education in Britain. The network of art schools created in the second half of the nineteenth century was directed from South Kensington and much is still with us today, nurturing the creativity for which Britain is renowned, in art, design and related 'creative industries' such as cinema and popular music. In 1843 there were six branch schools (in Manchester, York, Birmingham, Sheffield, Newcastle upon Tyne and Spitalfields in London); by 1869, 107 had been established. The Museum's library was crucial to Cole's nationwide ambitions, and lent books, prints, drawings and photographs to the new regional art schools. It was especially close to his heart, since, unlike his early colleagues, he had not worked as a curator, artist or art historian. Instead, he had proved himself as a reformer of the Public Record Office, before becoming Prince Albert's right-hand manager of the Great Exhibition.

One of Cole's sternest critics was Ralph Wornum (1812–1877), who began writing for the *Art Journal* in 1846. Wornum published an *Outline of a General History of Painting* in 1847 (which as *Epochs of Painting* became the standard art-school textbook) and was appointed a lecturer on Ornamental Art at the Government School of Design in 1848. Wornum believed that every workman should be 'a man of taste . . . capable of fully appreciating the spirit of his pattern'.[19]

Cole was shrewd enough to read Wornum's articles and then hire him, as the first full-time librarian.[20] In 1852 Wornum opened the Library to the public, especially to working designers. Also at Marlborough House, a study room was set aside for photographs, plaster casts and electrotypes, all curated as part of the Library's resources. To facilitate access, Wornum started to catalogue the Library's collections by subject. In his *Prospectus* (1853) he described the Library as 'consisting at present of about 2,000 volumes, portfolios of prints, drawings &c relating to decorative art and ornamental manufactures'.[21] By the time his catalogue appeared in 1855,[22] the Library had expanded to 5,550 volumes along with 100 portfolios of prints and drawings.

To structure the Library's collections, and hence (quite literally) how one could approach the history of art and design, Wornum adopted the system of 30 'classes' that had been devised for the contents of the Great Exhibition of 1851. His aim was not that of a historian, attempting to articulate the anatomy of the history of art and design, but rather that of a librarian alert to the need to provide swift access to the most relevant material for readers' needs. Wornum was convinced that the Library could be a catalyst for design reform. To that end, as the *Prospectus* proclaims, the Library offered 'a range of subjects directly bearing upon upwards of two hundred trades now carried on in the metropolis'.

As both Librarian and Keeper of Casts, Wornum also published an illustrated catalogue of the casts after Renaissance ornament.[23] His dual role reflects the significance of the Library as a visual resource. Like the illustrated books, prints, photographs, brass rubbings and other reproductive visual material in the Library, plaster casts formed part of the surrogate collections gathered to compensate for the young museum's limited holdings of unique historic objects and to open doors among students and working craftsmen to the wider world of art and design.[24] As Wornum stated in the *Prospectus*, 'it is intended to be an Art Manufactures Library of the most comprehensive character practicable ... while the Museum is necessarily extremely limited in many respects, the library is in a measure infinite ... It is the experience of the world pitted against that of an individual.' He hoped that here artists, craftsmen, 'the skilled workman or practical mechanic might receive a ray of light'.[25]

A colourful personality as well as a prominent writer, Wornum must have presented Cole with a rival in terms of public profile, especially when the new design school, public galleries and library at Marlborough House proved popular. According to William Bell Scott, Wornum was 'a Hercules in muscular development, and he married one of the most perfectly formed and most beautiful women in London'.[26] He also fathered 14 children. After three years with Cole he left Marlborough House to become Keeper of the National Gallery in 1855. From 1859 to 1860 he installed the National Gallery's six rooms of British paintings at South Kensington, including the bequests of J.M.W. Turner and Robert Vernon.[27]

The Art and Design Library

In 1857 the Museum, School and Library moved to the V&A's present location in South Kensington. Cole declared: 'Other collections may attract the learned to explore them, but these will be arranged so clearly that they may woo the ignorant to examine them. This museum will be like a book with its pages always open, and not shut.'[28] It was a revealing choice of simile. In promoting his museum project, Cole made many disparaging comparisons with the British Museum, whose library had opened to the public in 1759 but remained inaccessible to most.[29] Cole had appointed J.C. Robinson (1824–1913), Curator of the Museum of Ornamental Art at Marlborough House, in September 1853, and with the move in 1857 Robinson also took on responsibility for the Library.[30] Initially, as noted above, the Museum's library in South Kensington was located close to the entrance, which was then in the south-east corner of the site. In 1860 it moved to rooms facing into the Schools Court, off the west cloisters of the new North Court where casts were shown; these surrogate collections of objects stood logically adjacent to the visual reproductions held in the Library.[31]

Robinson is best known as a pioneer collector of both paintings and the applied arts, a man with a hunger for masterpieces for the Museum (and himself) who enjoyed adventurous shopping expeditions in Italy and Spain. After moving the Library to new premises in 1861, he published a catalogue the following year. It differed from Wornum's in being structured alphabetically by author. As a result, users required greater familiarity with the history of art and the applied arts. Unlike Wornum, Robinson did not write an introduction setting out the Library's aims, other than to state that the catalogue was 'for the use of the Students frequenting the Art Library and for the provincial schools which have the privilege of obtaining books on loan'.[32] In the Museum's tenth Annual Report (1862), Robinson is described as 'Keeper of the Art Library and Superintendent of the Art Collections'. Following disagreements with Cole, he was sacked in 1863 via the deletion of his post, but was nevertheless retained as a consultant 'second artistic referee' for his expert advice on acquisitions.

In 1864 Cole appointed the architect John Hungerford Pollen (1820–1902) as General Superintendent of Catalogues. Pollen commissioned a series of descriptive, illustrated catalogues to specific aspects of the Museum's collection that appeared through the 1870s – for example, Textile Fabrics, Ivories, Maiolica, Furniture and Woodwork, and Bronzes – then adapted their texts into elegantly designed shilling 'Art Handbooks' with copious woodcuts.[33] Pollen's first major project was a massive bibliography, the first instalment of which was published in 1866. The following year Robinson lost his job as a consultant.[34]

A 'Universal Catalogue' for an Encyclopedic Art Library

For Cole, the big lesson of the Great Exhibition was to think internationally. Its success (above that of traditional national exhibitions of manufactured goods held in Britain, France and Germany) lay in its near-global scope, thanks partly to the British East India Company as a principal exhibitor. Cole's next international endeavour focused on reproductions of works of art, as plaster casts, electrotypes, photographs and other media. In 1863 he declared the Museum's role was 'to make the historical and geographical series of all decorative art complete and fully to illustrate human taste and ingenuity'.[35] Clearly, Cole's priorities had moved on from just improving commercial product design to much broader aims. In this he may have been responding to the success of another legacy

of the Great Exhibition, the Crystal Palace as reconstructed at Sydenham with displays by his former colleagues Matthew Digby Wyatt and Owen Jones. For a busy man in a hurry, the historic collections could not grow fast enough if the Museum were to compete with new rivals and live up to Cole's latest ambitions.

Having first secured the support of the Government's Foreign Minister, in 1864 Cole promoted an 'International Exchange of Copies of Works of Fine Art'.[36] At the Paris Exposition Universelle of 1867, the tireless networker secured signatures from Europe's crown princes to 'The International Convention for Promoting Universally Reproductions of Works of Art'. This international exchange agreement led to the expansion of the V&A's collection of casts, which opened in its vast new courts in 1873. A parallel project of potentially epic proportions that helped to promote the young museum abroad was the *Universal Catalogue of Books on Art, Compiled for the Use of the National Art Library and the Schools of Art in the United Kingdom* (1870).

Robinson's catalogue of the Library took the form of a printed book, which went out of date immediately on publication because the book collections grew so much faster than others in the Museum. Rather than publish new editions each year, a strange solution was adopted: producing a 'universal catalogue' of every single book on art in print that the Art Library would ever hope to acquire. This was, of course, equally flawed thinking, for it suffered from the same incapacity to keep up with new publications and required the regular publication of supplements. But it was a brilliant marketing initiative. Cole had first promoted the idea in 1852 when he urged the British Museum to pursue it.[37] With the help of a Committee of Advice composed of 'upwards of 400 correspondents in different parts of the world',[38] along with a team of cataloguers, every bibliographic entry necessary was gathered to create the world's most complete bibliography on the literature of art. The first instalment, for the letters A to B, was published in 1866 in the advertisement pages of *The Times*, which soon proved too expensive. Cole included the first section among the Museum's publications in the Paris International Exhibition of 1867, where the display was awarded a medal by the exhibition jury. The first set of two volumes was published in 1870, edited by J.H. Pollen, and listed 14,794 titles. It claimed to include 'not only the books in the Library, but all books printed and published at the date of the issue of the Catalogue that could be required to make the Library perfect'.[39]

Through Cole's sense of ambition, the grand title 'National Art Library' was adopted by 1865,[40] and the re-branding was accepted immediately. In aspiring to be a 'universal' art library the scope of the collections now expanded beyond the priority set by Wornum on servicing London's designers. Indeed, to complement its surrogate collections, particularly of photographs, other 'universal' catalogues were compiled and published. These thick inventories of the world's treasures in public and ecclesiastical buildings seem now the art historical equivalent of Britain's global ambitions in its imperial age. As copies of these catalogues and inventories were sent to the regional art schools and acquired by art museum libraries abroad, so the scope of the history of art was defined and promulgated.

The international inventory research project was managed initially through the British embassies in Paris, Dresden, Berlin, Munich, Turin and Rome, and then by Cole's staff working from *Murray's Handbooks* for travellers (Cole's daughter Henrietta Lindsay Cole is credited as compiler and was paid by Pollen to work on the *Universal Catalogue*). Four volumes were published of the *Universal Art Inventory ... of Fine and Ornamental Art Executed before AD 1800 Chiefly to be Found in Europe*: for *Mosaic and Stained Glass* (1870), *Goldsmiths' Work, Enamels and Ivories* (1870), *Metalwork* (1876) and *Woodwork, Sculpture* (1879).

The National Art Library

Robert Henry Soden Smith (1822–1890) joined the Museum as an assistant to J.C. Robinson in 1857 to help curate John Sheepshanks's gift of paintings, donated to launch the National Gallery of British Art. Soden Smith then helped with a great loan exhibition in 1862,[41] while also running the Library (fig.3). He served as head of the Library from his formal appointment in 1867 until his death in 1890.[42] A noted collector of books, drawings, photographs and prints, especially of sixteenth-century German engraved ornament, Soden Smith was also a published poet and an expert on freshwater shellfish. He presided over the most significant period in the expansion of the scholarly collections and of the Library's premises.

Soden Smith may have been embarrassed by an anonymous celebratory article, 'The Art Library at South Kensington', that appeared in *The Builder* on 9 October 1869. It describes with relish the growth of the collections, systems of cataloguing and the services to readers. The combative tone of the comparisons with the British Museum's library suggests that Henry Cole may have been the author of this puff, perhaps to encourage Soden Smith in his new position. For example, it proclaims:

> Students who have become accustomed to the
> manipulation of the illegible temporary catalogues of the
> British Museum ... experience a pleasant surprise on their
> first occasion of consulting the Art Library at Kensington.
> The readers there do not appear to be considered in the
> light of intruders, of public enemies, or of ignoramuses....
> If the object of research be indicated, the officers of the
> library take an interest in aiding the pursuit. They seem
> to have not only a personal acquaintance, but an intimate
> friendship, with the authors whose works are on the shelves
> ... more information can be garnered at South Kensington
> in a day than at Bloomsbury in a week or more. The
> South Kensington staff, in a word, are not attendants,
> but assistants.[43]

In 1858 the Library curated 2,200 prints and drawings. By 1884 there were 65,000. Much of this came in gifts and bequests. In 1868 a collection of illustrated books was selected from the library of Chauncy Hare Townshend. In 1869 the

The new library was the first space in the Museum to be equipped with electric light as part of its fittings, rather than gas. It also faced north (like artists' studios) to provide an even amount of daylight, without the damaging effects of direct sunlight from the south. In his annual report Soden Smith praised the 'abundance of light, by which the smallest print can be read and colours distinguished'.[46]

The Architecture

The new library range was designed in 1876 by General Henry Scott and built from 1882 to 1884.[47] The basic form seems indebted to Wren's library at Trinity College, Cambridge (begun 1676), in the way it is raised above a cloister to avoid damp and fire. Unlike Wren's library, the books are shelved in a wall system rather than in bookcases at right angles to the walls ('stall system'). An upper gallery runs around all three rooms. This feature follows the Bodleian Library, Oxford (1610–12), the Hofbibliothek, Vienna (1722–6), and the British Museum's reading room (1854–6). It became common in libraries only after the Dresden librarian, F.A. Ebert, fell from a ladder to his death in 1834.[48]

In exterior elevation the Library follows the 'South Kensington style' (red brick with terracotta and mosaic decoration) that is traditionally traced to the architecture of Renaissance Lombardy for its source of inspiration. Cole and Scott may have also had in mind Ludwig I's library in Munich (1832–43), faced with red and yellow brick in the Italianate *Rundbogenstil* by Friedrich von Gärtner. The other recent precedent, the Bibliothèque Ste-Geneviève in Paris (1843–40) designed by Henri Labrouste, has an Italian Renaissance exterior with a vault of iron columns and arches within, which Labrouste used again for the reading room of the Bibliothèque Nationale (built 1865–8).

By comparison, the interior decoration of the National Art Library is almost austere, confined to the plaster overdoor reliefs by Reuben Townroe (fig.5), who also designed the 15 mosaic panels on the exterior. Fortunately, unlike in Paris, readers can look out of the window, past the terracotta

library of Alexander Dyce brought more than 14,000 books, manuscripts and drawings; in 1876 John Forster bequeathed more than 18,000 books and manuscripts, including five of Leonardo da Vinci's notebooks (as discussed in the following chapter). Located between the North Court and the Schools Court, however, the Library suffered from poor light and shortage of space, which, according to one journalist in 1870, 'nothing but the unusual urbanity of the Librarian and his assistants can render tolerable'.[44]

In 1884 Soden Smith moved the Library into its present suite of three purpose-built rooms and adjacent offices. At that time the Centre Room could accommodate up to 20 readers consulting or copying (for watercolours were permitted) large books and folios of prints, drawings and photographs. To that end it was fitted with desks of greater surface extent than those in the main reading room. Prints and large folios were stored and consulted in the West Room, while the Reading Room provided for up to 80 readers, just as it does today. Regular users in the later nineteenth century included the architect Philip Webb (who probably first introduced William Morris to the Museum) and Philip Burne-Jones (who much preferred it to the British Museum's reading room).[45]

fig.4. The Reading Room in 1899, with prints hung on the piers. The choice of the two prints flanking the main entrance, Raphael's *Sistine Madonna* (on the right) and Holbein's *Meyer Madonna* (both Gemäldegalerie, Dresden), must have been a tribute to the former librarian, Ralph Wornum, who identified correctly the version of the latter in Basel as the original in preference to the more famous painting in Dresden.

decoration of wise owls and the faces whose gagged mouths remind us of the need for silence (fig.2). Busts of eminent Museum directors, architects and curators survey the busy desks. On the Museum's ground floor, directly beneath the Library, a gallery provides a similar sense of cloisters to Wren's library at Cambridge. By 1900 it was serving as the 'Antique Cast Court'[49] and is now devoted to 'Sculpture in Britain'.

The Photographic Library

The V&A has the oldest and largest museum collection of photographs of the visual arts in the world. It began by 1853 in the Library, as one of the collections of reproductions assembled to supplement the Museum's historic objects. At first, the collection included only images of works of art, but it soon aspired to provide a 'universal' resource for visual research, while also representing the art of pioneer photographers such as Julia Margaret Cameron.[50] In 1856 Henry Cole appointed his brother-in-law Charles Thurston Thompson (1816–1868) Superintendent of Photography. When the Museum and Library moved from Marlborough House to South Kensington in 1857, there were already about 1,000 photographs. In 1858 alone it added a further 600. The following year the British Museum transferred its prints and negatives to South Kensington. Collecting accelerated through the photographing of loan exhibitions, through Cole's international exchange agreement of 1867 for reproductions (which included photographs as well as plaster casts), through buying and commissioning topographical surveys of India, Canada, the Cape and the Empire beyond, and through J.C. Robinson's purchases while collecting art abroad. By 1884 there were approximately 50,000 photographs; in 1908 there were 175,000; by 1927 the Library had grown to 250,000 images,[51] and by 1949 it held 300,000 photographs.[52]

In 1934 the photographic library recognized a drop in demand from readers, in part thanks to the availability of cheaper illustrated books, and so decided to specialize in collecting sculpture and architecture, rather than continue to acquire photographs for all categories. The 39 subject

categories ranged from Anatomy to Mural Painting, along with works by artists, shelved in file boxes. Like the universal inventory volumes published in the 1870s, its role in 1934 was still 'to provide a record [through photographs] of the chief treasures of the world, so that artists and others may see the best reproductions'.[53]

Other great photographic libraries were then emerging, ones that are in use today: at the Warburg Institute, the Witt and Conway libraries at the Courtauld Institute of Art, and at English Heritage (the former National Buildings Record of the Royal Commission for Historical Monuments for England). It has been argued that the idea of a library of photographic images as a research tool for the history of art was pioneered in Hamburg from 1889 by Aby Warburg and that, thanks to the move of his institute to London in 1933 (with Rudolf Wittkower as curator of photographic collections), 'the use of photography was, de facto, part of the inheritance that transferred to the UK'.[54] One precedent for all these was the photographic 'museum' of Baron Minutoli, a photographic survey of his collection published and distributed by the Minutolisches Institut in Liegnitz, Silesia, to aid the reform of industrial design. Prince Albert donated a set of 152 of Minutoli's photographs with printed text to the Library in 1855, and another volume of the same the following year.[55]

Following the establishment of a Photographs section in Prints, Drawings and Paintings in 1977, the remaining boxes of photographic images were distributed among the curatorial departments for their own research use. Photographs as museum objects are now also held by the Asian Department, by Theatre and Performance and elsewhere. Much of the collection of documentary photographs survives in the Museum's archives.

Reforms and 'Re-arrangement'

Robert Henry Soden Smith died in 1890 while in post. His successor, W.H. James Weale (1832–1917), was a leading scholar of early Netherlandish painting, and became Keeper in 1890 aged 58. He was described by Francis Haskell as having 'long been the doyen of the historians of early Flemish painting',[56] and he is now best known for his publications on Hans Memling (1901), Gerard David (1905) and Hubert and Jan van Eyck (1908). After a short career in teaching,[57] in 1855 Weale had moved to Bruges, where he became a champion of historic buildings at risk. Supplementing his private income as a dealer in antiquities, through his research in fifteenth- and sixteenth-century archives and publication of documentary sources Weale provided a foundation for the study of early Netherlandish art that still holds firm today. He advised on potential acquisitions long before joining the Museum's staff.

As with his predecessors in the Library, it was his background as an art historian, rather than as a librarian, that qualified him for the position and reflected the value placed on scholarship and on the Library's curatorial collections. Weale immediately recognized the inconvenience of adding to the *Universal Catalogue* each time a new title was acquired,[58] and so introduced a card-index system for the author catalogue, which survived until the Library started to computerize in 1987. He also established standard rules for cataloguing books. His other great contribution was as a collector, his most noted acquisition being the French missal of 1350 that he identified as from St Denis in Paris.[59]

Weale became 'the very type of the antiquary',[60] patriarchal in appearance, tall and lean with a full grey beard, bespectacled and shambling in his gait beneath sloping shoulders. According to one obituary,

> his naturally irritable temper could indeed blaze into a furnace of just anger; as when an unwary vendor of obscene prints who had penetrated to his room was pursued by him, shouting with fury, through the reading rooms. But the poor woman who brought him a Caxton, ignorant of its value, found in him a protector from the wolves of the world of books.[61]

In 1897 he was dismissed by the V&A's director for speaking too frankly to a Government Select Committee enquiring into the Museum's management. It was noted with outrage in *The Magazine of Art* that 'one of the few acknowledged experts within this institution, and a man possessed of a European reputation as a librarian of the first order .... received peremptory notice to quit'.[62] Nevertheless, the following year the Museum published his pioneering catalogue and history of bookbinding.[63]

fig.5. One of the plaster overdoor reliefs
in the Library, designed by Reuben
Townroe (1835–1911)

The Government Select Committee led to further reviews and the 'Re-arrangement' of the Museum's structure in anticipation of its reopening in 1909. This followed the vast expansion of the building, designed by the architect Aston Webb. He had conceived a grand staircase in the main hall (as in Alfred Waterhouse's Natural History Museum, which opened in 1881, on the opposite side of Exhibition Road) leading visitors direct to the Library, but this was never built. Nevertheless, ample space was provided for the Library as it spread, with a further 'Book Production Gallery' continuing west on the central axis (today Room 74).[64]

The west side of the garden (at the same level as the Reading Room) was devoted to the new Department of Engraving, Illustration and Design ('EID', later combined with the Department of Paintings as the Department of Prints, Drawings and Paintings), which was born from the National Art Library's graphic collections. Opposite, the east wing overlooking the garden was devoted to the Forster and Dyce collections of books, manuscripts, paintings, prints and drawings. The standing of these two bequests is further revealed by the evidence of staffing given in the Select Committee's Report (1898), which lists five Keepers: one for Textiles, one for the Art Library, one for the Circulation Department (responsible for travelling exhibitions[65]), one for 'Editorial work' and one for the Indian Section (the report comments: 'Among these Keepers one is in charge of Museum Publications, Dyce and Forster Libraries'). The Assistant Director had responsibility 'for Sculpture, Ivories and reproductions in Plaster'.[66] With this redistribution of responsibilities the Library was able to focus on the art of the book, and its services to readers and staff. Through a series of exhibitions in its new gallery, the Library shared its collections and expertise with the general public.

In its obituary of James Weale *The Times* noted that 'Mr Weale left his spirit alive in the younger men whom he had trained'.[67] George Henry Palmer (1871–1945) succeeded Weale as Keeper in 1897, aged only 26, having joined the Museum in 1889. Palmer survived the restructuring of 1898–1909 sufficiently well to serve the longest period as Keeper, 34 years, before retirement in 1931. As well as the exhibitions, his era is noted for securing George Reid's gift of 83 illuminated manuscripts. In his obituary *The Times* recorded that his keepership 'covered the scientific development in the history of art which marked the first quarter of the century'. Palmer kept the Library up to date with the latest publications. It remained open during the First World War, when he served with the army in Alexandria, rose to the rank of major and 'notably distinguished himself by his imperturbability in the bloody landing at Sulva Bay' (the Gallipoli campaign, 1915).[68]

Albert van de Put (1876–1951) joined the Library in 1895, aged 19; he trained under Weale and served as Keeper from 1931 to 1936. Put became world renowned for his knowledge of heraldry, with an expertise key to identifying arms on silver, in paintings and elsewhere. In an article in 1935 he summarized the Library's holdings as:

> designed to meet the requirements of, on the one hand, the several kinds of practitioners in art (non music) as well as architectural and art students, designers, typographers, theatre artists, and graphic artists; and, on the other, of art historians, archaeologists, aestheticians, art critics, and collectors; nor are such subjects as museology and art in commerce overlooked. Of equal importance are the facilities it affords the Museum staff for reference and research.

He also announced that 'a comprehensive series of facsimiles of old master drawings and engravings, and of other works of art, is available. Native literature on Far Eastern and Indian art is represented.'[69]

Through the Second World War

Philip James (1901–1974) was appointed Keeper in 1937. While Deputy Keeper (1936–7) he organized an exhibition on contemporary graphic design that captured the moment. It also strengthened the Library's Trade Literature collection, devoted to the art of advertising. James spent only two years as Keeper before wartime secondment took him to the Ministry of Home Security. He did not return to the Museum when the war ended but became Art Director of the Arts Council.

From 1939, through the war and until 1962, Arthur Wesley Wheen (1897–1971) served as Keeper. Following heroic service in the First World War,[70] he had settled in England, from Australia, in 1919 as the University of Sydney's Rhodes Scholar at Oxford. Wheen is best known as a translator of German war novels, including Erich Maria Remarque's *All Quiet on the Western Front* (1929).

In his memoirs of his time as Director of the National Gallery, Kenneth Clark recalled: 'During the war the National Gallery, by means of the concerts, the War Artists exhibitions and the exhibitions in the basement, had "kept going" when other museums and galleries were completely out of action.'[71] In fact, the V&A's library remained open to the public in London during the Second World War, as it had in the First.[72] The only other museum services available in London were the libraries of the British Museum and the Science Museum.[73] Before reopening in November 1939, in preparation for the London Blitz, treasures such as the Da Vinci notebooks, the St Denis missal and the manuscript of Charles Dickens's *David Copperfield* were moved into a bombproof crypt; other precious material from the Library was evacuated to Montacute House in Somerset. By now the subject indexes had assumed great value as the world's largest classified bibliography of art literature, so they were microfilmed and a copy sent to Washington DC for safekeeping in the Library of Congress (fig.6).

In 1942 R.A. Butler, head of the Board of Education, provisionally agreed with the V&A's Director, Sir Eric Maclagan, that the Warburg Institute would merge with the V&A. As part of this attractive plan, the Warburg's director, Fritz Saxl, offered the services of his staff to reorganize the collection of photographs in the V&A's library. The Warburg Institute was housed across Exhibition Road at the Imperial Institute from 1938 to 1958 and was incorporated into the University of London in 1944.[74]

Arthur Wheen would have been party to these discussions. A friend of Herbert Read (a former curator at the V&A), Henry Moore and T.S. Eliot, Wheen was an avid collector for the Library of material on Picasso. He must have enjoyed the controversial exhibition *Picasso Matisse*, held at the V&A in 1945. Writing in 1949, Wheen was confident that the National Art Library was 'now the largest specialised collection of art literature in the world' and he defined its role more broadly than ever before, as 'for the study of the history, philosophy, technique and appreciation of the arts'.[75]

Wheen's successor, John Harthan (1916–2002), joined the V&A from Cambridge University Library in 1962. A scholar as well as a professional librarian, he produced important works on illustrated books and bookbindings.[76] Harthan was succeeded in 1976 by Ronald Lightbown (b.1932). An authority on Italian Renaissance painting and sculpture, Lightbown translated and published in facsimile *The Three Books of the Potter's Art* (c.1557) by Cipriano Piccolpasso (1524–1579) of Castel Durante, the classic Renaissance technical treatise on ceramics, the manuscript of which J.C. Robinson had found in Florence and purchased for the Library.[77]

The New Art History and New Readers

According to Harthan's obituary in *The Times*, in the 1960s most students in the Library 'were practical art students who came to make copies of illustrations and for whom jam-jars full of water were laid on'.[78] This all changed in the following two decades. During the 1970s the amount of publications on art increased dramatically, prompted by the scale of 'blockbuster' exhibitions and their catalogues, by the advent of colour television with series such as Kenneth Clark's *Civilisation* (1969) and by the rise in demand for art history and art and design at undergraduate and postgraduate degree level. The V&A itself launched an MA course in the History of Design with the Royal College of Art in 1982. Like the V&A's galleries and exhibitions, art and design became more intellectually attractive to students and academics in the 1970s and 1980s. The 'New Art History' asserted a more interdisciplinary frame

of reference and global scope, embracing issues familiar to students of material culture, sociology and anthropology.[79] As a consequence, the range of readers expanded.

The number of researchers using the Library increased further in the 1970s and 1980s with the ambitious growth of the London auction houses (Christie's, Sotheby's, Bonhams, Phillips) and the ambitions of art dealers to publish catalogues with pages of ever-more detailed scholarly descriptions. With the advent of the Sotheby's Institute (founded 1969) and Christie's Education (opened in South Kensington in 1978), their students also became regular users. The National Heritage Act (1983) gave the V&A trustee status and also led to the founding of new public bodies including English Heritage, Historic Royal Palaces and the Heritage Lottery Fund, all of which needed new professional recruits. This boom in the 'heritage industry' further increased demand on the National Art Library from the 1980s.[80] As the average age of readers dropped, so the atmosphere of the reading rooms quietly changed, as the minds of some younger readers strayed away from their texts. According to the *Daily Telegraph* several years later, the V&A was voted 'the nation's most romantic museum'.[81]

With Roy Strong as Director from 1974, the V&A reaffirmed its commitment to contemporary art and design. In 1977, 300,000 photographs from the Library's collections were selected as art objects, given their own curator and transferred to the Department of Prints, Drawings and Paintings.[82] The following year the Archive of Art and Design (AAD) was founded to fulfil a 'new policy of making the National Art Library a repository for primary source material on the fine and decorative arts'.[83] The AAD collects material produced by British artists, designers, makers and firms since the nineteenth century and of societies and institutions, for example, the archives of Heal's. While the art and design museum approach favours examples for their aesthetic and/or technical qualities, for the AAD the integrity of the archive group is respected. Building on a long-established tradition of rescues, this initiative began by bringing together material already held by various departments across the V&A. It soon attracted a large number of gifts, and today the AAD provides a national service, giving advice on the most suitable location for such papers. This was an era, however, when Government cutbacks had a direct impact on front-line services in the Library, which led to complaints in the press from some of its eminent readers.[84]

Ronald Lightbown was the only Keeper of the National Art Library to move on to run another V&A department. In 1985 he became Keeper of Metalwork, a field in which he was already an acknowledged authority. His wide range of expertise encompassed Italian Renaissance sculpture, French goldsmiths' work and jewellery. In that year Roy Strong appointed as 'chief librarian' Elizabeth Esteve-Coll (b.1938) from the University of Surrey's library. Soon the wooden drawers of the card index of authors, shelves of subject catalogues and carousels of microfiches were replaced by computer terminals. Finding that the Library's 'role was merely that of a Department of the Museum', she resolved 'to re-establish it as the "heart and core" of art library provision in the UK ... as a training centre for art librarianship'.[85] Following her promotion to Director of the V&A two years later, Esteve-Coll recruited her successor, Jan van der Wateren (b.1940), from the British Architectural Library at the Royal Institute of British Architects. He continued her internal reforms while forming leading collections of contemporary book art and comics.[86]

One consequence of this change in professional perspective was a growing conviction that the National Art Library had outgrown the V&A. In 1997, when the British Library finally departed from the British Museum, the trustees of the V&A were persuaded to start seeking a new home elsewhere in London for the Library. According to a pamphlet published by the Museum in June 1997, signed by the chairman of the V&A's trustees, for readers,

> the facilities which they find at the Library, and the efficiency of the services which they are offered, are far more important to them than the matter of whether the Library is located in SW7 or WC2.... it is a matter of balancing the convenience of a small number of specialist user groups with the prospect of a much improved service.[87]

With hindsight, it is surprising to see the changing profile of the readers at that time described as 'small ... specialist user groups', especially since they included the V&A's own staff. This departure would have also meant the removal from the V&A of the historic collections of the art and design of the book and publishing, together with the divorce of illustrated and fine printed books from the prints and drawings collections.[88] Fortunately, the policy was dropped.

The Twenty-First Century

As part of a wider review and merger of the curatorial departments, the V&A decided to find an appropriate partner for the Library. Following van der Wateren's retirement in

2000, the process of reintegrating the National Art Library with the Museum began by joining it to the Department of Prints, Drawings and Paintings (PDP).[89] This department already specialized in an integrated approach to the graphic arts, deploying the range of its collections in exhibitions such as *Dickens* (1970) and *Byron* (1974).[90] After settling on its new name, Word and Image was launched in 2003 by its Keeper, Susan Lambert, a specialist in prints and contemporary art and design; she retired in 2005. The new department was more than a matter of administrative efficiencies; it confirmed the V&A's conviction that the graphic arts and the Library belong together as one collection, integrated with exhibitions and permanent displays throughout the Museum.[91] Today, this merger of the National Art Library with PDP feels like an inevitable and happy reunion. The choice of name reflects the commitment to the interrelationship of visual and verbal communication through the graphic arts; it also challenges librarians, curators, archivists and other staff to think laterally together across all the collections, particularly when planning displays, exhibitions and publications.

A Resource for Creativity

In the twenty-first century the V&A has rediscovered its founding objective: to be a vital source of inspiration for everyone, not only artists and designers but also the general public, for we all affect the design of our daily worlds through our economic power as consumers. The National Art Library shares in that ambition once again by seeking to expand its community, to be a key resource to curators and art historians as well as to the heirs to those Victorian craftsmen, people that together are now called the creative industries.

The V&A's library currently attracts 42,000 reader visits each year, 64% of which are from students, academics and curators. The other 36% includes art dealers, journalists, designers and art researchers. Among the latter the Library is today a crucial resource for film-makers and television production companies, particularly those working on costume dramas such as *Downton Abbey*. They order up illustrated books from the eighteenth and nineteenth centuries on cosmetics, wigs, underwear, even tattoos. Some seek not only visual information but also actual objects to replicate as props in their films, such as the earliest copies of *Vogue* and *Country Life* magazines. For everyday ephemera, historic publications record in their advertisements the kind of household goods that are rarely preserved by museums. Designers of dresses do not come only from the world of period costume dramas; one regularly recognized reader is Vivienne Westwood.

Another group within this current research community is genealogists. Seeking evidence of their ancestors through retail catalogues, many researchers are drawn to the V&A's specialist collection of publications from the World's Fairs. Descendants of medal winners seek images and descriptions of their ancestors' inventions and commercial products. In this age of digital research, when so much literature is now scanned and available online, some question the need for physical libraries. But when it comes to *visual* research, of images not words, the software has yet to be perfected that can pinpoint an image in the way search engines can find the words or the names you want.

The Library markets itself as a resource to students newly arrived in London (especially to the art colleges, such as the Royal College of Art, Central St Martin's and Camberwell School of Art) through presentations and social media. Artists and graphic designers are particularly attracted by the V&A's annual Illustration Awards, with an exhibition and cash prizes for book covers, book illustration, editorial illustration in periodicals and (most valued of all) the Student Illustrator of the Year. Around the Museum at any one time 250 books, pamphlets and manuscripts are on rotating display throughout its galleries, including one former reading room which doubles as a display of part of the V&A's general twentieth-century collections. Here younger visitors often gasp as they enter the grand purpose-built Victorian library and pull out their smartphones to take 'selfie' photographs next to walls of books. Some recognize the Library from its frequent use by film crews.

So while the V&A's library continues to provide a world-class research service for curators, art historians and the art trade, it is also returning to its founding aims: to be a source of knowledge and inspiration to the world of art and design, to support London's role as a centre of the creative industries. Since most readers stay for an average of three hours (longer than visitors to major exhibitions) one could claim that the Library is the best-used space in the Museum. It certainly has the best-known groups of visitors, the V&A's diverse research community.

This book is published to accompany an international touring exhibition marking the first decade of the Word and Image department. The project seeks to raise awareness of the collections and the themes they can illuminate in the history of art and design through their integrated display. It also develops the next generation of staff with personal expertise in the art and design of the book and publishing – staff who are committed to the delivery and display of such material to the V&A's audiences worldwide. Today, just as the V&A is so much more than a museum, so Word and Image is even more than a library, print room, collections, archives and galleries. Online, the V&A's combined resources and the paths they open up now reach beyond Henry Cole's vision of a 'universal' catalogue of books and encyclopedic collection of reproductions. Since many of the Museum's knowledge services are now delivered online, there are immense opportunities to reach much broader audiences, but also great challenges with the increase in user expectations and demands. Nevertheless, in the Library resources must remain focused: on complementing the collections and subject areas served by the V&A, and on the representation of books and other publications in the Museum's history of art and design.

Set at the heart of the 'world's leading museum of art and design', this wellspring of both information and inspiration is a key to fulfilling the V&A's mission: 'to enrich people's lives and inspire individuals and everyone in the creative industries, through the promotion of knowledge, understanding and enjoyment of the designed world'.[92]

Verzierung eines Kreutz Gewölbes in der Halle
der Villa Madama.

Décoration d'une Voute d'arête du Portique
de la Villa Madama.

The Growth of the Library Collection 1837–1909

ROWAN WATSON

Mechanics' Institutes, funded variously by benevolent patrons, employers or the workers themselves, were the most successful educational institutions that developed in early nineteenth-century Britain.[1] The vice president of the London Mechanics' Institution, Charles Toplis, was among witnesses called before the Parliamentary Select Committee on Arts and Manufactures in 1835. The Committee was sufficiently impressed by Toplis to include his paper on the functioning of his institution in its report.[2] It is clear that this model, with its lectures, supervised instruction and a library, lay behind the Government School of Design that opened its doors in 1837. The School had a troubled history in its early years, with lack of agreement about its real nature, but an undoubted success was in the library that it brought together, the nucleus of what from 1865 was to be called the 'National Art Library'.

Training Artists and 'Ornamentists' at the Government School of Design

The superintendent of the Government School, until his resignation in 1843, was the brilliant William Dyce (1806–1864), an artist later to become Queen Victoria's favourite painter and adviser to Prince Albert. There were very different views about how to train artists destined to work in industry. For most of the trustees of the School – MPs from an industrialist background supplemented by Royal Academicians – figure drawing was the basis of all art (the London Mechanics' Institution had classes for 'Drawing the human figure'). Dyce, on the other hand, after a tour in Germany, felt that the workshop was the proper place to train artists working in manufactures, not an art school, where training axiomatically involved figure

drawing and composition. Dyce insisted that there were two kinds of artist, those devoted to the fine arts and those who were 'ornamentists'. Appropriate for the latter was Dyce's programme of teaching, which involved prescriptive copying of geometric shapes before proceeding to drawing stylized ornament based on natural forms. But figurative art did find a place in the School's programme of instruction. Dyce recognized that 'ornamentists' as well as fine artists had to learn the lessons of fine art, defined as art dealing with 'history, poetry and generally with moral expression'. Both ornament and fine art aimed at beauty, and no beauty was possible without principles drawn from the natural world.[3] So from its inception the Library collected materials relevant to both fine art and ornament. With model books and drawing manuals were books on art and art theory, on topography, natural history, costume and anything else that the fine artist or the jobbing artist might require. Dyce subtly inserted his view in the device he designed for the title page of the drawing manual he provided for the Government School. This device showed a Raphaelesque angel in inspired mode drawing with a stylus; underneath was a citation in Greek from Aristotle's *Nicomachean Ethics* suggesting that real knowledge could be gained only by actually doing and making (by implication in a workshop).

The design reform movement that produced the South Kensington Museum after the Great Exhibition of 1851 promoted ornament as a new category of art, and Raphael, recognized as the supreme exponent of Renaissance art, was called on to be its patron saint, around whom all could rally. In 1843 the facsimile made by Richard Evans of Raphael's ornamental panels in the Vatican had been acquired for the new School after the Treasury made available a special grant for the stupendous sum of £510.[4] Collecting photographs of Raphael's drawings was to be a priority for the new museum and its library after 1855. In that year, the extraordinarily large sum of £122 was paid at the Bernal sale for a maiolica plate thought to represent Raphael painting a ceramic (V&A: 1717–1855), though the Museum wisely hesitated to confirm the subject matter. And from 1865 the cartoons made by Raphael for the making of the Sistine Chapel tapestries were lent by Queen Victoria to show in the Museum's galleries, where they remain to this day.

The Library had two divisions. The Central Library at the Government School presented itself as a source of designs and images.[5] Its holdings were described as 'Books of Plates of Ornament'. Works providing models predominated, with architectural history and ornament having pride of place. Though there were books by the antiquarian Henry Shaw on medieval artefacts and, for instance, the three volumes of Chapuy's *Moyen-âge monumental* (1843–6), works on Roman and Greek art were much preferred. There was a handful of antiquarian books – a copy of Alciati's famous emblem book, but in a French edition of 1559 rather than the original of 1531; Pierre Bourdon's *Essais de gravure* of 1703; and the 1729 edition of Palladio's *Five Orders of Architecture* as revised by Colen Campbell – but collecting focused on modern publications. Significant for the future were books that can be seen only as models for illustration: the 1840 edition of the *Nibelungenlied* with woodcut illustrations after Bendemann and Hübner, and a 'Book of German Ballads' recycling German prints with images and texts illustrated by 15 artists, both of them acquisitions responding to new fashions in contemporary art in England. An illustrated edition of Thomas à Kempis, printed in Vienna in 1839, was catalogued as 'Ornamented Woodcuts', doubtless a source to which students following the School's classes in wood engraving were directed.

The School's Lending Library had a very different flavour. It catered for a broad education in art and literature, at both a popular and a scholarly level. Next to classical works of English literature, starting with Shakespeare and Milton, were works of a theoretical nature, among them the discourses of Sir Joshua Reynolds, the lectures on sculpture by John Flaxman and Edmund Burke's treatise on the sublime. With drawing manuals and standard art historical texts, there were the mass-distributed works that were so popular in the 1830s and after, such as the *Penny Encyclopedia*, *Chamber's Encyclopaedia* and the publications of the *Library of Entertaining Knowledge*. Perhaps telling of the readership for which these works were intended was the presence of John Walker's *Critical Pronouncing Dictionary*, reprinted many times after its appearance in 1791.

Developing an Encyclopedia of Antiquities, Art and Design

Books in the Government School library were intensively used: what survived formed the basis of the Library housed with the Art Division in Marlborough House by the new Department of Science and Art after the Great Exhibition of 1851.[6] From a library for training designers, the Library became, under Ralph Wornum, an extension of the Museum, allowing coverage of its subject areas encyclopedically by including facsimiles (published and unpublished) in the form of prints, drawings, books and photographs as well as original works. From the outset, no prior knowledge of the literature on any subject was assumed of its users. The Library's printed catalogue of 1855 took the form of a bibliography under a number of subject headings that agreed, where possible, with the classes of exhibits in the Great Exhibition.[7] Wornum was pleased that 'out of the whole 30 classes . . . no less than 24 classes [in the Library catalogue] are immediately interested in matters of art and taste, over and above the mere mechanical skill implied in their avocations', since workmen had to produce objects 'administering to intellectual as well as material wants'. Appropriate works were listed under each heading, many of them appearing under several. Subject catchwords were scattered throughout, so that under 'Decoration' could be found, for example, headings for 'Anglo-Saxon', 'Norse' and 'Saracenic Ornament' with multiple cross-references. The great scholarly multi-volume enterprises of the nineteenth century were now represented, from Silvestre's *Paléographie universelle* (1839–41), J.B. Seroux d'Agincourt's *L'histoire de l'art par ses monuments* (1823) and Willemin's *Monuments français inédits* (1828–39) to Alexandre Lenoir's *Musée des monuments d'Agincourt* (1800–6), Alexandre Du Sommerard's *Les arts du moyen âge* (1838–46) and the colossal *Description de l'Egypt* in 23 volumes (1809–28), put together at Napoleon's command.

Under Wornum the presence of antiquarian books increased: the Nuremberg Chronicle of 1493 appeared under 'Costume' and under 'Engraving' (fig.8); the *Arte de escrevir* of Francisco Lucas of 1577 and writing books by Anton and Johan Neudörffer of 1601 and 1631 under 'Alphabets'; under 'Antiquities' were references to Godoy Ponce de León's *Antiguedades y excellencias de Cordova* of 1627 and William Dugdale's *Antiquities of Warwickshire* of 1656. Given the Library's interest in book design, it is worth mentioning that in the section 'Manufactures – Printing' (corresponding to Class XVII of the Great Exhibition) were the chromolithographed illustrated books of Noel Humphreys and Owen Jones, which had been greeted as technological marvels of book production. 'Buildings, Engineering, Surveys and Carpentry' formed one section, whereas the heading 'Trades', the last section, was reserved for works on specific kinds of product, from bookbinding and clockmaking to calico printing and shoemaking. Sections in the catalogue of 1855 under 'Art' on Taste, Theory and Art History developed what the Government School library had held on matters relating to fine art and aesthetics. All this involved much repetition, with the same title appearing under many headings. The *Catalogue of the Art Library* of 1861–2, by 'J.C. Robinson, Curator',[8] resorted necessarily to a purely alphabetical sequence by author or title, albeit heavily sprinkled with subject headings that gave cross-references to relevant works. The subject approach – so significant an educational tool, as Wornum put it in 1855, for an art manufactures library serving 'artisans and even

manufacturers' – led to the pioneering series of subject bibliographies that appeared from the mid-1870s and the handbooks with historical introductions on categories of object collected by the Museum.

These catalogues, of bleak utilitarian aspect, rather hide the nature of the growth of the Library collections. Works acquired on botany, on natural history and on geology were legion. Authorities from William Dyce and Owen Jones to Richard Redgrave and Christopher Dresser had all stressed that the origin of good design began with the study of organic and natural forms. All agreed with Dyce's proposition that 'the ornamentist is an imitator of nature' and that beauty in works of industry is achieved because they follow 'the same principles as the works of nature themselves'. The collections contained sources on which artists doing any form of work could rely. In an age that prized realism and scientific accuracy in images, artists had a resource that enabled them to meet any client's expectations. There were works on the costumes of Native Americans and Tuscan farmers as well as on German matrons and Parisian dandies; travel books with images of subtropical forests as well as Scottish highlands; historical and contemporary accounts of furniture and cooking utensils as well as gardens and interior decoration.

Even before the project that began in 1865 to compile a universal catalogue of works on art there was an effort at completeness. The acquisition registers and the reports made by the Art Library show an astonishing growth, on the one hand compiling a visual encyclopedia of everything relating to art and design in its widest sense, and on the other attempting to collect the major works of antiquarian scholarship both of the nineteenth century and earlier. Students using the reading rooms were directed to classified lists to identify their requirements. Much non-book material was too disparate and came in such overwhelming bulk that it had to be treated differently. From 1860 separate registers were kept for drawings, engravings and photographs, showing the multifarious ways by which material was acquired: by commission, by gift and by purchase.

Drawings

The register for drawings gives a vivid account of the sources from which material was acquired. Much was bought from the German scholar Ludwig Grüner, resident in England from 1841 to 1857. He was based in Dresden from 1858 but kept regular contact with England and with Queen Victoria and Prince Albert, whose artistic adviser he had been from the days they had begun decorating Buckingham Palace and Osborne House on the Isle of Wight. Grüner supplied original drawings – for instance, a sixteenth-century design 'in the manner of G da Udine' in 1857 – but mostly facsimile hand-painted or hand-drawn copies of designs and architectural ornament. In 1859 he was paid £31 for 'A set of drawings of the "Scaffale" in the sacristy of Santa Maria in Organo at Verona'. In 1866 and 1867 he supplied 'drawings illustrative chiefly of brick architecture in Northern Italy'.[9] In March 1880, two years before his death, he was paid £100 for a collection of 83 drawings of Italian decoration and mosaics. The work of celebrated designers was sought out, so that 1,001 initial letters designed and illuminated by Owen Jones were acquired in May 1864. Beyond this, the original artwork for Jones's *Grammar of Ornament* had been seen 'hanging in the architectural museum' in 1859 and was quickly transferred to the Art Museum, to join the Library in 1861; it was noted later that the 100 drawings had cost £105.[10] Homage was paid to Jones after his death by the placing of a mosaic portrait in the east cloister of the Museum, suitably dressed with an academic gown and a portfolio under his arm.[11]

Photographs

Photographs were collected in abundance, both to supply accurate copies of the artefacts in which the Museum was interested and, from an early date, as substitutes for paintings and drawings, so that landscapes, portraits and figurative scenes taken by the new technology joined the Library collections. Thus in August 1862 photographs of the articles in the Madras Exhibition of 1857 taken by Captain L. Tripe were received from one Dr Hunter, while in the same year the Museum photographer, Charles Thurston Thompson, handed over photographs of Raphael drawings in the Devonshire collection at Chatsworth. Thirty-five photographs of architectural monuments in Paris and other French cities were bought from Edouard-Denis Baldus in March 1858. It can be difficult to determine whether works were acquired as documentation or as works of art in their own right. Photographs of the Crimean War by Roger Fenton might fit into the former category (though today considered as art photography), as might landscapes that complemented the huge number of topographical books. The Library did not follow Ruskin, who in correspondence with Peter Henry Emerson in 1886 counted photography among 'the arts of idleness'.[12] Portraits and other works by Julia Margaret Cameron were admired by Henry Cole, who not only acquired them for the Museum but also ensured that an exhibition of her work took place in 1865. These were doubtless considered the equivalent of artworks: some were gifts but many were bought, from the art dealer Colnaghi, for prices of between £1 and £2 each. The price alone was sufficient to differentiate them from documentary material acquired at the time – perhaps Cole was then sensitive to portraiture. Samuel Redgrave, who in 1865 had organized a loan exhibition of more than 3,000 portrait miniatures, was charged in that year to organize a series of truly colossal loan exhibitions of national portraits, almost all paintings, in the Museum, intended to illustrate British history from medieval times and the progress of art in Britain. Each painting was photographed by the Museum. A set joined the Library's collections and copies of the 2,085 photographs involved could be bought by members of the public for 1s. 6d. each.[13] Interest in photography as a new medium also meant that many of the first books illustrated with photographs were sought out to join the Library collections.[14]

Engravings

Registers for 'engravings' describe materials printed with very different techniques. Engravings owned by the sculptor

Sir Richard Westmacott RA (1775–1856) were bought in July 1857 for the not inconsiderable sum of £81 7s. 6d.; pasted into the eight albums were 644 prints after works by Raphael, Rubens, Titian and others. At the same time an image of the Jesse window at Chartres Cathedral, chromolithographed by E. Beau, was acquired. A series of 23 prints by Aldegrever was transferred from the Art Museum to the Art Library in 1856, with the note that they had been purchased from Evans & Son, a dealer who must have counted the Museum among his most regular customers, on 14 October 1855. There was as well a collection of 32 'Impressings [rubbings] from engraved metalwork' and reproductions of 'Frescoes in the Hofcapelle in Munich, painted by Hess and his pupils, lithographed by J.G. Schreiner'. Contemporary work was not excluded. The *Illustrated London News* in 1848 ran a series of illustrated articles on the history of wood engraving that later appeared as a book by W.A. Chatto: the prints were bought by the Library in 1868 for £12 12s. as examples of contemporary engraving. The problem of keeping up with the rate of acquisition became clear in the 1880s, and from 1885 prints, drawings and photographs had their own dedicated series of inventory numbers. For images of a secondary nature – either cheap prints or prints cut out of nineteenth-century magazines – a 'tear-sheet' collection was made, organized by theme, from literary narrative to architecture, the latter arranged by county or region; this collection was still being added to after 1900 and today occupies some 200 boxes.[15]

Collecting Historical and Contemporary Materials

From 1855, when Wornum left to become Keeper of the National Gallery, to 1863, direction of the Library fell to the Keeper of Art, J.C. Robinson, one of the most remarkable scholars of the nineteenth century. Robinson termed the Library a 'Central Library', and provided further materials for a circulating library whereby the Library's 'Works of Art' could be lent to the provincial art schools that were springing up all over Britain – this mirrored what the Art Museum was doing. Books had been displayed at the Great Exhibition of 1851 (the

catalogue indexed 'Bookbinding' and 'Books' between 'Bonnets' and 'Boots') and Robinson had a certain sympathy for the book as an object worthy of study, even if there was uncertainty whether the Library or the Museum was its proper host. In 1856 he declared that 'the artistic embellishment of books displayed in specimens of ornamental binding, chiefly of ancient periods, and in every variety of illuminated, engraved, and typographic ornament' was a subject to be covered by the Museum, but went on to announce that it was to be served by 'the acquisition, at a relatively very slight cost, of a numerous series of examples', the examples turning out to be leaves cut from complete books, both manuscript and printed. By 1856 these leaves were already circulating to provincial art schools in five sets of enormous wooden frames. Cuttings, easily found in the art trade and antique shops of Europe from the 1830s, were acquired by Robinson's successors as examples of design important for students who would end up in the printing industry; they were acquired in large numbers – some 4,000 by 1900.[16]

Robinson was reluctant to acquire complete illuminated manuscripts or printed books through fear of duplicating the collections in the British Museum library. Such complete manuscript codices as were acquired can usually be shown to be interesting for their binding or illustration. But the demands of scholarship and the proper understanding of museum objects required works that today would be put in the category of 'Early Books' or 'Rare Books'. Robinson's special interest was in works of the Italian Renaissance that explained how objects were made – and in this he set up a line of collecting that carries on to the present. His great coup came in the winter of 1860–1, when he managed to bring away from Italy the celebrated manuscript by Piccolpasso of *c*.1557 that gave a detailed account of how the most decorative ceramics of the Italian Renaissance, maiolica, were made, this at a time when the Museum's collections of these wares were growing apace.[17] Pagano Paganini's work on mathematics, *Divina proportione* (Venice, 1509), with its diagrams by Leonardo da Vinci, was bought in 1863, and by the end of the century the Library contained, among other works on science and technology, Vannoccio Biringuccio's manual on metal-working, *De la pirotechnia* (Venice, 1540); Georgius Agricola's work on the mining, refining and smelting of metals, *De re metallica* (Basel, 1561); Wenzel Jamnitzer's still unpublished manuscript treatise of 1585 on scientific instruments and their use for goldsmiths' work, geometry and astronomy; and Jacques Besson's pioneering work *Le Cosmolabe; ou, instrument universel* (Paris, 1567), together with a densely illustrated German translation of his work on engineering devices and machines, the *Theatrum instrumentorum et machinarum*, of 1595.

There was initially confusion about what was appropriate for the Art Museum and what for the Art Library. The inventories of the Art Museum published from 1860 include a number of bindings, early printed books, books bought at the Paris Exposition Universelle of 1855, manuscripts (European and Persian) and miniatures cut from manuscripts. These materials were in due course – after Robinson's departure from the Museum – passed to the Library. Bookbindings, so important for students as showing the application of flat pattern to what was by the 1850s a mechanically produced article, were acquired by the Art Museum until 1867, after which only the Library acquired them (but those in materials other than leather became museum objects, so that the ivory covers of the celebrated Lorsch Gospels, made in the ambience of Charlemagne's court *c.*810, are in the Sculpture Collection[18] and the dazzling embroidered binding done for an eighteenth-century Italian archbishop is in the Textile collection). The collection was to grow hugely, particularly in the mid-1880s, when collections of rubbings of bindings were also bought – from W.H. James Weale, a scholar who in 1890 became head of the Library and whose catalogue of 1898 of the Library's bindings, none of them dating from after 1800, remains a landmark in the study of the subject. In the next century, in 1940, Henry Clements (1869–1940) bequeathed to the Library his collection of British and Irish armorial bookbindings, some 965 in all, dating from 1550 to 1890, covering more than 90 per cent of all known such works.

Early Imprints

A few early printed books in the Library were inherited from the Government School, and a few were bought thereafter, for example, a copy of Lomazzo's celebrated treatise, the *Trattato dell'arte de la pittura* of 1584, acquired in June 1854 (a copy of the 1585 reprinting, heavily annotated by Inigo Jones, was bought in 1994 [fig.13]). But it was left to Robinson's successors, in particular Soden Smith ('Provisional Librarian' of the National Art Library in 1866 but Keeper from 1867), to add early imprints to the Library collections. Acquisition of books by celebrated printers and from famous printing centres was first reported in 1870, when books from the presses of Nicolas Jenson in Venice of 1476 and of Peter Schoeffer in Mainz of 1477 began a series that amounted to more than 100 incunables by the end of the century (the number was to rise to 172 in the next century). Illustrated versions of European classics of the sixteenth and seventeenth centuries were collected with enthusiasm; the Library thus holds multiple illustrated editions of Ariosto and Dante, for example, and works of Ovid so necessary for understanding the art production of the *ancien régime*. But it was not until 1908 that the first editions of Vasari's famous *Lives* of painters and sculptors, of 1550 and 1568, were acquired, modern versions sufficing until then.

Illustration

During Robinson's period as Keeper of Art, the Library began systematically collecting books illustrated by British artists (fig.7). In 1858 a committee was set up to make 'a Collection of Illustrations of the British School of Engraving'. Apart from Robinson, the committee was made up of Sir John Hippesley Bt,[19] the engraver George Thomas Doo RA, and Richard Redgrave RA, by then Surveyor of the Queen's Pictures as well as Inspector General for Art, responsible for the teaching curriculum of art schools throughout the country. The committee doubtless had the approval of Henry Cole, who as 'Felix Summerley' had published books illustrated by well-known artists. It was a natural adjunct to the arrival in South

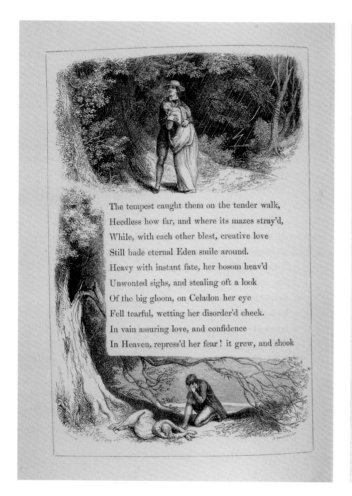

Kensington in 1857 of the Sheepshanks Collection of British Paintings, brokered by Redgrave and given to the Museum to form the nucleus of a National Gallery of British Art. This was a serious venture. A gallery was erected to receive the pictures, and beyond that galleries were constructed for the Robert Vernon Collection of paintings by contemporary British artists and the Turner Collection, both owned by the National Gallery. The new museum realized Sheepshanks' vision for a National Gallery of British Art. Although the National Gallery recalled its Turner Collection in 1861 and the Vernon Collection in 1876, Constable's daughter, Isabel Constable, was moved in 1888 to give the Museum nearly 400 paintings, drawings, sketches and watercolours done by her father.[20] Sheepshanks's bequest had included watercolours, regarded in the nineteenth century as a quintessentially British art. In 1860 Mrs Ellison donated 51 watercolour paintings (with a promise of 50 more) 'to further the formation of . . . [a] national collection'. Illustration needed the same treatment, and it may be that Robinson's initiative was prompted by reflections on the state of illustration in the 1850s. If one excepts national heroes like Turner, the illustration that was commercially successful before the 1860s was lively, anecdotal and marked by caricature, eminently suitable for a popular market and claiming Hogarth and Rowlandson as its mentors – one recent authority has aptly characterized the images of Hablot Browne ('Phiz'), Cruikshank and others that helped sell the novels of Charles Dickens as 'knockabout'.[21] From the mid-1850s the mood changed: illustration was to be judged by the criteria applied to painting. The wildly successful illustrated periodicals of the 1860s commissioned images that were improving and morally uplifting, and satisfied everything that could be expected from celebrated painters. For John Everett Millais, made a Royal Academician in 1863, for instance, book illustration became an important source of income. It may be significant that the former kind of illustrator barely appears in Robinson's catalogue of books of 1861, whereas Royal Academicians and safe, conventional artists like Birket Foster do: the celebrated Moxon Tennyson of 1857, with its illustrations by Pre-Raphaelite painters, was included, but the periodical *Punch*, at this date, was not. The single-leaf material registered as engravings only partly compensated for these omissions.

The importance accorded illustration appears in Robinson's catalogue of the Library of 1861,[22] where illustrators' names appear as headings, so that the heading 'Turner' provided cross-references to all the books he had illustrated – this system for identifying illustrated works was maintained for major figures in the *Universal Catalogue of Books on Art* of 1870. The Library was to be the natural home of illustration, the publishing industry being one of the chief employers of artists. Illustrated books from Britain, continental Europe and North America were collected in abundance. Publishers of *Punch* and the *Illustrated London News*, both founded in the 1840s, needed teams of illustrators and wood engravers for the images they carried, but the cheap 'impulse-buy' magazines like *The Graphic* (from 1870), which sold largely through their pictures, required regiments of such people. Their achievement was celebrated at the V&A in 1901 with the *Loan Exhibition of Modern Illustration*, which despite the title nevertheless included a high proportion of work in the Museum's library collections to document illustration since the 1860s. From the mid-1850s photography had been crucial for the swift production of wood engravings and electrotypes: the artist's image was transferred to the block, enlarged or reduced, by photographic processes for the wood engraver to work on. The proofs and the artists' designs became collectable items, and the Library acquired quantities of both.

The exhibition of 1901 appears today like a swansong of nineteenth-century technology, celebrating an age before plates for printing could be produced directly from a photographic image (a development that by 1890 John Ruskin was fortunately not in a state to witness and rail against). Books advising artists how to make their artwork suitable for reproduction by the printing industry abounded in the decades around 1900 and all were acquired by the Library as a centre for illustrators. Typical of the genre were Joseph Pennell's *Pen Drawing and Pen Draughtsmen, their Work and their Methods: A Study of the Art To-day with Technical Suggestions* (London and New York, 1889), Henry Blackburn's *The Art of Illustration, with Ninety-Five Illustrations, and an Appendix Explaining Four Processes and a List of Process Block Makers* (London: W.H. Allen, 1894) and Joseph Kirkbride's *Engraving for Illustration: Historical and Practical Notes, with Two Plates by Ink Photo Process and Six Illustrations* (London: Scott & Greenwood, and New York: Van Nostrand, 1903). From the 1880s Dalziel & Co., ever eager to have their work in national collections, sent the much-prized 'burnished proofs' of their work to the Library; engravings after images of Millais, Luke Fildes and others were accessioned in 1904 as having been specially taken under the personal supervision of the Dalziel Brothers at the Camden Town Studio 'before the woodblock was sent to the printer', a standard of excellence for students. By that time the Library had proofs of work by, for example, Sir John Tenniel for *Alice in Wonderland* (by the Dalziel Brothers, 1872) and proofs for images in *Punch* (by Swain, 1860s). In 1899 the widow of Randolph Caldecott sold a collection of 320 pieces of artwork (mostly proofs) by her husband to the Library; she may have been guided by the example of the widow of George Cruikshank, who in 1884 and 1887 had been in a position to make a gift of her husband's artwork, which included drawings as well as proofs, to the

fig.9. Illustrated catalogue of Silber
& Fleming Ltd, Manufacturers
and Wholesalers (London, c.1880)

Library. If the underlying aim of nineteenth-century collecting of illustration was governed by an awareness of the technical competencies illustrators might need, the situation was rather different at a later date: T.M. MacRobert's survey, *Fine Illustrations in Western European Printed Books* (London: HMSO for the V&A, 1969), focused above all on illustration as art.

Like the Museum, the Library received support from many quarters in the nineteenth century. Gifts made to the Library indicate what its benefactors felt was its role, and explain as well aspects of its collection strengths.

Donors: Manufacturers

Among the first supporters of the Library were manufacturers. As regards books, the family firm of Leighton & Co., for instance, was a regular donor. This company had perfected a means of producing case-bindings with ornamental designs in colours and gold stamped on cloth, and was naturally keen to have its works represented as examples of manufacturing excellence. John Leighton (1822–1912) was a prolific designer who worked under the name 'Luke Limner'. From the company in 1853 came a gift of paper-hanging (i.e. wallpapers) and specimens of bookbinding. In the 1860s John Leighton's name appears regularly among lists of donors to the Library. Other kinds of manufacturer sent in their catalogues, and it seems that many were retained and passed into the Library at various dates. Today, material of this kind is known as the

Trade Literature Collection.[23] The firms that exhibited at the Great Exhibitions in London sent in their promotional catalogues and pamphlets, as did firms such as Minton, Doulton, Wedgwood, Silber & Fleming and Dixon & Sons from the 1860s. Many were densely illustrated. The fourth edition of *Macfarlane's Cast Iron Manufactures*, for example, proudly boasted its medal gained at the International Exhibition of 1862 on its title page; balcony railings, tables, chairs and ornamental pipework were among articles available, the last illustrated bedecking a fine Renaissance castle (fig.10). The advent of the department store was, of course, accompanied by densely illustrated catalogues. That of Silber & Fleming, which joined the Library in 1898, came in two volumes, each with more than 500 illustrated pages, many of them in colour (fig.9). The catalogues of retailers supporting progressive contemporary design, like Heal's and Liberty's, which both served customers sympathetic to Arts and Crafts ideals, were acquired selectively as they were published. As the Museum's new materials-based departments after 1909 extended their documentary resources, a more systematic approach was adopted. The first catalogue of Liberty & Co., the leader of Arts and Crafts design on the high street, was acquired in 1881, but a complete run came in 1975 when the Museum held an exhibition to mark the company's centenary. Today, individual items of this kind are recorded on the Library's catalogue, so that pamphlets in, for example, the Ecko Collection (bought in 1993) advertising wirelesses of the 1930s, fridges of the 1950s and electric fires of the 1960s are readily identified.

The Library's role as amassing documentation about the world of goods and design in the contemporary marketplace, in conjunction with the Museum's departments, led to the establishment of the Archive of Art and Design (AAD) in 1978.[24] In the course of their research, Museum curators had amassed – and identified the whereabouts of – quantities of primary sources relating to the history and practice of subjects from ceramics and furniture to metalwork production and textiles. Much of this material risked destruction. The AAD allowed whole archive groups relating to designers,

fig.10. From the catalogue of
Macfarlane's Cast Iron Manufactures,
4th edn (Glasgow, *c*.1863)

MACFARLANE'S EXAMPLES, *showing various modes of applying Pipes, &c., to Buildings.*

artists, businesses or organizations to be acquired, stored
and catalogued effectively. Among early donations were the
archives of Heal & Co., with catalogues, business records,
photographs and other promotional materials, the order books
of Holland & Sons Ltd, cabinetmakers, and the records of the
metalwork manufacturer and electroplater Elkington & Co.

Donors: Artists and Engravers

The 'artistic skill and feeling' of John Thompson (1785–1866)
as a wood engraver was celebrated in the obituary that
appeared in the *Art Journal* on his death. In 1857 he had made

a substantial gift of more than 400 woodcuts to the Library.
In an age when critics attributed the quality of prints to the
skilled hand of the engraver as much as to the artist providing
the design (Ruskin published diatribes against 'hasty and
cheap expedients' in the engravings used by the popular
press),[25] Thompson was an authority. He had won a gold
medal at the Paris Exposition Universelle of 1855, and had
been employed by printers in London and Paris to reproduce
designs by artists as famous as Edwin Landseer, Paul Delaroche
and Horace Vernet. He was among the founding fathers of the
Museum in that from 1853 he ran classes in wood engraving

in Marlborough House, teaching both men and women and gaining commercial commissions for his students. One of his sons, Charles Thurston Thompson, after training as a wood engraver, became the photographer of the new museum in 1856 (evidence of the significant link between wood engraving and photography). Another son, Richard Thompson, worked in an administrative role and was Keeper of the Educational, Food and Animal Products collections from 1859 – these were appointments that no one dared to suggest had a link to their father's friendship with Henry Cole. John Thompson's widely reported series of lectures on the history of the craft was a standard point of reference. His gift included the 34 woodcuts of Albrecht Dürer's *Passion of Christ* series, as well as work by Lucas Cranach and images from the *Nuremberg Chronicle* of 1493, but his main concern seems to have been to endow the Library with the best modern work, some of it by Thompson himself but also by his British contemporaries, his teacher Robert Branston (1778–1827) among them, and German work by Robert Reinick (1805–1852), Gustav Richard Steinbrecher (1828–1887) and others. It was the presence of such works and such an authority in South Kensington that doubtless led firms such as Dalziel and Swain to donate examples of their own woodcuts later in the century.

Donors: Collectors

Major gifts were received in 1868, 1869 and 1876 from three individuals, all from the same social circle, gifts that denote support of the educational aims of the new museum and its library. As it happens, all three were associates of Charles Dickens. Chauncy Hare Townshend (1798–1868) was the dedicatee of *Great Expectations*, whose author honoured – with some groaning – the request in Townshend's will to make coherent and publish his notes on religious matters. Townshend had set up a charity with Angela Burdett-Coutts, who had worked with Dickens to similar ends, to give 400 children free evening education in Westminster. His will stipulated that the South Kensington Museum could select what works it wanted from his collections, Wisbech Museum

being the residuary legatee. The librarian, Soden Smith, selected more than 350 books (from a library of some 7,000 volumes), all of them remarkable for their illustration. There were books illustrated by Bewick (to join those already in the Library), Audubon's *Birds of North America*, the Bible with Doré's illustrations, works by Byron, Bunyan, Goldsmith and others, and books illustrated by the likes of Cruikshank and Gavarni. Townshend's library also included a large collection of photographs – only Prince Albert and Queen Victoria rivalled him as collectors of early photographs. Thanks to Townshend, the Library could add landscape photographs by Gustave Le Gray and Camille Silvy, as well as Roger Fenton's pictures taken during the Crimean War, to its resources. All complemented the collections that the Library was building up.

Alexander Dyce (1798–1869) similarly sympathized with the new museum's mission to serve working people. His library, unlike that of Townshend, was kept as a distinct entity within the South Kensington complex. It was rich in English literary texts, from Elizabethan and Jacobean drama to eighteenth-century classics, all of them works that complemented the literary diet offered to students by the Library since the days of the Government School of Design. Part of its value today is that the books are mostly in their original format, giving (like the library of John Forster) pristine examples of Victorian binding and book design.

The bequest of John Forster (1812–1876), handed over by his widow shortly after his death, followed that of Dyce in stipulating that his collection should remain as a distinct entity (fig.11). Though famous for its 'Autograph collection' with letters of Queen Elizabeth, Charles I and Civil War leaders, quite apart from a fifteenth-century Book of Hours, notebooks of Leonardo da Vinci, the correspondence of Samuel Richardson and David Garrick, notebooks and diaries of Jonathan Swift, corrected proofs of Samuel Johnson's *Lives of the Poets* and the manuscripts of all but two of the major novels of his friend Charles Dickens, the value of Forster's library lies in the picture it gives of a Victorian man of letters very much engaged in the issues of the day.[26] A vast

collection of pamphlets provided source materials for the
histories he wrote of Civil War leaders, from Oliver Cromwell
to William Laud, but it also covered contemporary debates,
including those on Abstinence and Art to 'Youth (Intellectual
improvement of)' and a text by the Revd Zincke on 'Why we
must educate the whole people'.

These personal libraries were part of much larger
collections. Townshend's collection included a very large
number of oil paintings, the greater part by Continental
artists (Canaletto, Cuyp and Rubens among old masters,
and a larger number of 'Modern Foreign Artists'), but also
by British artists (Constable, Danby, Etty, Fuseli); oil paintings

were dwarfed in quantity by watercolours and drawings where those by British artists outnumbered those by contemporary foreign artists. Townshend's collection of precious stones, mounted on rings, remains one of the glories of the Museum, with diamonds acquired from the celebrated collection of the banker Henry Philip Hope (1774–1839), important in that it pre-dates nineteenth-century habits of artificially enhancing the qualities of gemstones.[27] Dyce's oil paintings were less distinguished, but among his voluminous number of drawings were works by Rembrandt and Rubens, and his collection of engravings, while showing a love of Hogarth, was centred on Michelangelo, Raphael and Rubens, a very conventional taste for his time. Dyce was something of a connoisseur: with more than 4,000 gems, coins and medals, he owned a carved portrait of 'An aged warrior', described as the work of an unknown Italian artist of the eighteenth century but today attributed securely to Baccio Bandinelli (1493–1560). Portraits of theatrical personalities were in abundance. Forster's small collection of oil paintings (48 in number) was dominated by modern British artists and included the celebrated portrait of Dickens done by Frith in 1859 (fig.12); this was also the case with his watercolours and engravings.

These major bequests were made to support an institution that was providing an education in art and design to a new audience, identified as 'artisans and the working population' as well as the general public. However much Charles Dickens might poke fun in *Hard Times* at the teaching programme at South Kensington, he was in total accord with its philosophy of making educational resources available to the common man.[28] When Enid Du Cane gave to the Library in 1913 a collection of books, drawings, pamphlets and photographs she had inherited from her uncle, the archaeologist and trustee of the National Gallery Sir Austen Henry Layard (1817–1894), she was satisfying the wishes of a man who had obtained parliamentary grants for workmen to visit the Paris Exposition Universelle of 1867 and publish reports, and who himself had taken 2,000 of his Southwark constituents to visit the exhibition at his own expense.

John Jones (1798/9–1882), his fortune made in the clothing industry and from contracts to supply army uniforms, amassed a huge collection of furniture, miniatures, pictures, Sèvres porcelain and ornamental works of art before his death in January 1882. Some two years earlier, he had decided after careful consideration that all were to be bequeathed to the South Kensington Museum, it being their most useful home. The pictures, with their examples of contemporary British painting, and the eighteenth-century French furniture, 'the greatest public collection of French furniture outside France',[29] effectively complemented Museum collections. In addition, Jones gave some 780 books, along with more than 300 prints and engravings. These reflected very much his personal interests. He had the first three folio editions of Shakespeare's complete works, perhaps the most studied books in the English language and still to deliver information about

Shakespeare and his environment. The title page of the third folio, of 1664, is inscribed with the autographs of more than 12 celebrities, from William Wordsworth to Charles Dickens. To have a Shakespeare first folio was de rigueur for a collector of Jones's stature.[30] His chief interest was in French eighteenth-century art, so that a volume of engravings by the mistress of Louis XV and doyenne of eighteenth-century French taste, Madame de Pompadour, published posthumously in 1782, was doubtless close to his heart; one can imagine that it vied in his affections with the furniture he thought associated with Marie-Antoinette. Jones's collection of playbills from Covent Garden of 1818–19 with advertisements for Mozart's *Marriage of Figaro* and Rossini's *Barber of Seville* show another aspect of his interests.

Donors: Scholars

When the *Universal Catalogue of Books on Art* was published in 1870, the literature on art was taking on a new character. The assumption that art was to be evaluated by its effectiveness as an agent of morality, taste and design excellence was tempered by a more historical and critical approach, one that, for historical works, prized the dissecting of archival and other primary sources. Emilia Strong (1840–1904) had been a student at the South Kensington Schools before her marriage in 1861 to the elderly Oxford don Mark Pattison (once thought to be a model for Dr Casaubon in George Eliot's *Middlemarch*); here she narrowly failed to gain women the right to attend life-drawing classes (she had to take them privately). She represented in fact a growing class of student, recruited from well-off families who could afford the fees to attend day classes – many feared that such students would predominate over those actually working in manufacturing. Ruskin, who had recommended that she attend the school in South Kensington, was offended by Emilia Strong's questioning his view that 'the poor must be well off . . . before the arts can become great', even though he might sympathize with her activities to promote trade unions. Writing as E.F.S. Pattison, her publications – based on systematic research in libraries, archive repositories,

museums and private collections – made her a major authority on French Renaissance art even before her second marriage, to the controversial Sir Charles Dilke, in 1885. In bequeathing her research library to South Kensington, with nearly 650 books dating from the fifteenth century to the twentieth, she was following the example of her husband's father, Sir Charles Dilke (1810–1869), whose name appeared regularly as a donor of books to the Library from the 1860s. Dilke's major donation in 1867 of books and pamphlets relating to the Great Exhibitions of 1851 and 1855, together with the series of gifts from Henry Cole and his son Alan Cole (1846–1934), lie behind the Library's magnificent collection of publications about the International Exhibitions of the nineteenth century and later.

Donors and Advisers: Curators

Since the Museum's earliest days, its staff acquired materials that they passed into the Library. Most noticeable perhaps are those in manuscript format. There was no real concept of a manuscript collection in the Library before the 1970s, though the nature of illumination as an art practice ensured that illuminated manuscripts were considered as a discrete category of object. In 1863 a manuscript report by Gottfried Semper dated 1852 on 'Practical art in metals' (the germ of his influential work *Der Stil in den technischen und tektonischen Künsten* of 1860–63), written for Henry Cole,[31] and a report of 1857 by A. MacCallum on a study trip in Italy in 1857, were passed to the Library after they had lingered in a curator's office, as were the records of the Society of Painters in Water Colours for 1808–25 in 1868. Such manuscripts were scattered around the library shelves until brought together in the twentieth century as a collection that now includes a rich assemblage of correspondences, treatises, diaries and other manuscript works relating to the history of art and design. The research of curators was frequently the path that brought such materials to the Museum, and many were passed to the Library after resting in a curator's office for some research project. The records of the frame makers and art dealers John Smith & Sons, dating from 1812 to 1924, were given to the

Library in 1936 by a friend of the last surviving owner of the firm through the good offices of a curator, who recognized their extraordinary value for throwing light on the art market of the time (fig.14).[32] As a market developed for documentary manuscripts in the twentieth century, the Library acquired, often at the behest of a curator, manuscripts such as the inventory of the home of a Paris lawyer, Gaspard Le Vasseur, of 1708; a treatise on calico printing at Merton Abbey dated 1792 by John Leach; the day-books and correspondence of Robert Bowman, a journeyman furniture maker, covering 1833 to 1852; and a group of letters to Frank Pick, the manager of design for London Transport in the 1930s.[33] The same principle operated with the archival materials that found their way into the Library's Archive of Art and Design. Many archive groups were gathered by a curatorial department and passed to the Library for cataloguing and public access, examples being the House of Worth records for 1889 to 1952, the Cecil Beaton papers bequeathed in 1986 and the Gaby Schreiber archives, 1940–89.[34]

Collecting the Contemporary around 1900

The Museum's library escaped the mistrust of those critical of the kind of art education promoted by teaching at South Kensington. Hubert von Herkomer, for instance, may have been driven to set up his own art school at Bushey in 1883 after finding both the South Kensington Schools and the Royal Academy Schools unsatisfactory, but it is clear that for artists as different as Walter Crane, Kate Greenaway and Beatrix Potter it was a major point of reference. Philip Webb and Edward Burne-Jones were both regular users,[35] while for the alumni of the Royal College of Art, as the Museum's art school became in 1896, it was the giant to which their own college library was a satellite. The matter of art and design has never been free of political animosities and radical disagreement. Exposure to international art movements such as Symbolism and Art Nouveau, quite apart from Modernism, provoked some unusually violent reactions. Walter Crane in 1911, for example, called Art Nouveau a 'strange decorative disease'. In 1916 the critic Marius Vachon singled out Art Nouveau and

Impressionism as styles which represented French cultural as well as military weakness, seducing France away from the Gothic and the art of the *ancien régime* in the eighteenth century which was the source and expression of its strength.[36] How did the Library cope with conflicting ideas of what was appropriate as resources for students and public?

If parts of the Museum found Art Nouveau problematic,[37] the Library was keen to give access to it. It acquired before 1900 Eugène Grasset's *Histoire des Quatre fils Aymon* (1883), a work that had great impact on book design and illustration on account of a novel way of colour printing but also on account of its design. Other works by Grasset were acquired that used the fount he had designed, and several of his posters were acquired in the sales of French poster art that took London by storm in the years 1896–8.[38] The same can be said for another designer whose reputation rivalled that of Grasset, Alphonse Mucha. These posters attracted a cult following in France, and the Library's acquisition on publication of, for example, Ernest Maindron's de luxe book *Les affiches illustrées 1886–1895* (1896) with its 64 colour lithographs shows how closely the phenomenon was followed in Britain. The corresponding avant-garde works published in England, such as Arthur Mackmurdo's *Hobby Horse* (1886–92) and *The Dial* (1889) by Charles Ricketts and Charles Shannon, were similarly made available in the Library on publication. The works of that *enfant terrible* Oscar Wilde were likewise soon in the Library collections, as were works illustrated by Aubrey Beardsley. For the latter, the advocacy of Gleeson White in *The Studio* had not rid him of undesirable associations. For many, he was the epitome of decadence, dangerously associated with French Symbolism and with Wagner – one should not read too much into the fact that Adolphe Jullien's laudatory work on Wagner of 1886, with 14 original lithographs, 4 etchings and 120 engravings, and the much less respectful book by the scholar-journalist John Grand-Carteret, *Richard Wagner en caricatures* (1891), were acquired only in the twentieth century.[39] Apart from illustrated books, Beardsley's drawings for Malory's *Morte d'Arthur* were bought from the bookseller Tregaskis

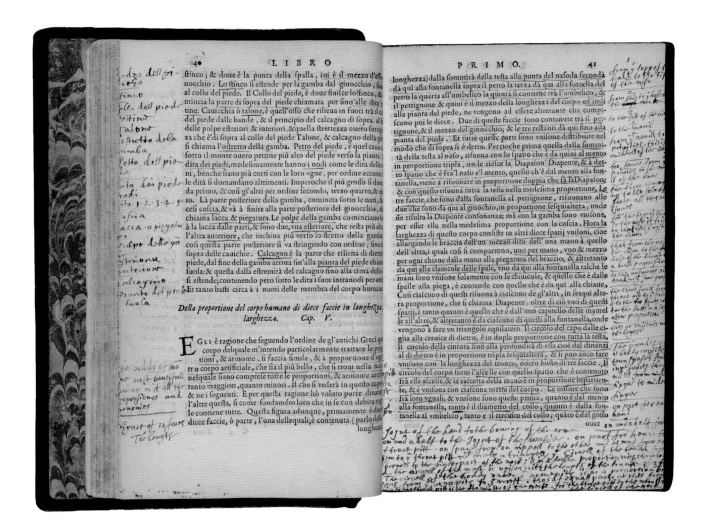

in 1899 for the enormous price of £27 along with a large collection of proofs from the widow of Gleeson White (for £4 4s.). The most influential historical work, much admired by artists and designers as varied as Edward Burne-Jones, Aubrey Beardsley and Walter Crane, was probably the 1499 edition of the *Hypnerotomachia Poliphili*, with its elegant woodcut illustrations;[40] there were two copies in the Library by 1886.

Perhaps the most inventive publishing of the late nineteenth century was that of William Morris's Kelmscott Press, Morris being a celebrated designer by the time he began

the business in 1891. His firm had designed one of the Museum's refreshment rooms at the beginning of his career in the 1860s, and he acted as a consultant ('Art Referee') over a number of acquisitions, so for the Library to take out one of the first subscriptions to the Kelmscott Press was natural. In typical Morris fashion, he investigated the qualities of all materials that make up books and had them made by hand, from paper and ink to typefaces and woodblocks – though it took his mentor, Emery Walker, to persuade him finally that electrotypes could match hand-engraved woodblocks

for ornament. The Kelmscott 'idea' was much copied. Just as there were book clubs in France that financed de luxe books illustrated by famous artists, so in Britain individuals and groups set up what are commonly referred to as 'private presses' in the Kelmscott tradition, each reflecting the taste and political alignment of its owner.

Illuminated Manuscripts and Cuttings

This *fin-de-siècle* development of the Library collections evidences a real change in the nature of the works collected, clearly seen with illuminated manuscripts, works that Ruskin and William Morris had discovered with such enthusiasm early in their careers. Before the 1890s such works had been collected at South Kensington as sources of design, usually acquired in bulk as fragments from dealers. But from the arrival of James Weale in 1890 single manuscripts and cuttings were acquired as individual works of art, expensive and of outstanding quality. Such, for example, were a miniature by Girolamo da Cremona, priced at £100, one of a number of cuttings bought from Charles Fairfax Murray in 1894; the St Denis missal of 1350, one of the great manuscripts of fourteenth-century France bought for £185 in 1891; and the Piccolomini Pliny, made in Rome in the 1460s, bought in 1896 for £300 – sums unheard of in the Museum thus far for such materials. With the arrival of the 83 illuminated manuscripts donated in 1902–3 by George Reid, a manufacturer from Dunfermline, and the six superb manuscripts left to the Museum by George Salting with his bequest of 1910 the Library had examples of the finest production of the medieval and Renaissance centuries. Such works were admired by Symbolist writers and poets, but a critic like Roger Fry was clear that late medieval and Renaissance works, so numerous in the Library, were quite meretricious. The simple Romanesque ornament he so admired was a new taste promoted by avant-garde modernist designers and architects. It was barely reflected in the manuscripts collected by the Library. The Victorian nature of the manuscript collection was also marked by the absence of

manuscripts in humanistic script from Renaissance Italy – the Piccolomini Pliny was in this script, but it was left to James Wardrop after 1945 to add an impressive series of such works, with the signal achievement of acquiring no fewer than four manuscripts by the celebrated scribe Bartolomeo Sanvito in superb humanistic and italic scripts.[41]

Whatever the arguments that surrounded the reorganization of the V&A in 1909, the Museum was recognized and envied throughout the world for its outstanding collections and for its educational activities. Its library constituted one of its chief glories. The *Burlington Magazine* called it 'a magnificent library … unique of its kind'.[42] No other museum library, from Prague to Chicago, Boston to Bombay, offered artists, designers and the interested public such an extensive and conveniently catalogued collection of historic and contemporary publications on art and manufactures, to be consulted in such an easily accessible and pleasant reading room.[43] Quite apart from purchases, the contacts of curators, the exchange agreements with museums internationally and the steady flow of gifts, had brought to the Library since its foundation an unrivalled corpus of material on the decorative and applied arts. From 1909 this was available next to the Book Production Gallery, which gave a detailed account of the art of the book through the ages.

Collecting the Art and Design of the Book after 1909

ELIZABETH JAMES

At the V&A, the twentieth century may be said to have begun in 1909, with the completion of the great Aston Webb building, its 720-foot (219.5-m) frontage, grand entrance and lantern dome. The new building prompted a 'Re-arrangement' of the Museum's collections and administration. Among other developments, the Prints and Drawings section of the National Art Library was promoted to departmental status, while the Library was at last provided with a large gallery of its own. Here, like the other curatorial departments, it was to display 'a reasonably logical scheme illustrating the technical and artistic development of the particular industry'.[1] The Library's 'particular industry' was 'Book Production'.

The display was broadly divided into three, for manuscripts, books and bindings. Illuminated manuscripts and printed books were arranged in geographical and chronological sequence, but topical cases with changing displays also focused on subject strengths. A large selection of printed lettering and writing manuals, especially Venetian, indicated how design underlay handwriting that in turn influenced typography. Early printed herbals were prize examples of books whose charming images served a function, of identifying the required plant. Pattern books, such as those for lace, were crucial resources for designers, and also made a highly attractive display. Publications on the decorative arts included those by designers themselves, such as Chippendale, Sheraton and Hepplewhite. The riches of the documentary manuscripts, both artists' letters and items from the literary collections, were also generously represented in the gallery.[2]

As discussed in the previous chapter, the Library had been acquiring books that reflected the design debates of recent decades, and the new gallery had a generous series of cases reserved for 'Modern' books and 'Modern presses', both British and foreign, with the Kelmscott Press having its own cases. In one respect the Committee of Re-arrangement had pointed the Museum back into the previous century, recommending that it should refrain from collecting 'modern specimens': objects less than 50 years old.[3] The core function of providing a working reference library meant, however, that 'any rule against the inclusion of modern specimens must obviously be relaxed in regard to books'.[4] The Library's collecting policy was expressed in a nutshell in the V&A's first *Review of the Principal Acquisitions* (1911):

> The principal aim of the Library is the acquisition, for the use of readers, of the more important new books on fine and applied art, produced in this country or abroad. At the same time, attention is given to acquiring such older books as fall within its scope.[5]

Library reports before and after 1909 tended to comment that the priority necessarily given to new works precluded much antiquarian collection-building. The bulk of retrospective special purchases would be documentary, especially manuscripts, or items such as rare trade catalogues. Conversely, however, the Library was relatively free to acquire contemporary 'specimens' of book art alongside informative literature. This chapter focuses on the Library's curatorial collecting and its engagement with modern and living practitioners from 1909 to the present.

Traditional (P)arts of the Book

As the leading English Arts and Crafts bookbinder and printer T.J. Cobden-Sanderson pointed out, in a book that was on display in the Library's gallery when it opened, 'The ideal book is a composite thing, made up of many parts.'[6] The parts of book production as exhibited in the new gallery were defined as: 'lettering, writing, illumination, types, type-ornaments, the arrangement of lettering on a page, the arrangement of the ornament or picture on a page, pictures as decorating the page of a book not as illustrating its subject, and book bindings'.[7]

It was recognized that the Library's collections of books and manuscripts were still 'intimately connected' with the prints and drawings still adjacent in the Department of Engraving, Illustration and Design (EID), and expected that the Library exhibition would be arranged in consultation with the Keeper of the new department.[8] EID was likewise exempted from the '50-year rule' since 'the specimens require little storage room and illustrate important developments of process which may soon become difficult or costly to procure'.[9] The division between page decoration and subject illustration is not hard and fast. The Library continued to collect books of illustrated literature, while EID began actively acquiring designs, proofs and examples of 'book decoration' alongside the interpretative illustration in its explicit remit. The two collections are profoundly complementary.

Calligraphy was fundamental to the Arts and Crafts Movement. Cobden-Sanderson had declared, 'It is the function of the Calligrapher, to revive and restore the craft of the Printer',[10] instancing as ever the example of William Morris. A case of recent works on lettering was displayed in the Book Production Gallery, including the latest edition of a handbook of alphabets written by the Library's curator, E.F. Strange: this was the book that just over a decade earlier had introduced Edward Johnston to lettering by modern designers, helping to set the direction of his career.[11] Sir Sydney C. Cockerell, collector and Director of the Fitzwilliam Museum, presented to the Library the manuscript 'Book of Sample Scripts', which he had commissioned from Johnston,[12] as well as correspondence

and documents including annotated copies of Johnston's seminal book *Writing and Illuminating and Lettering* in each edition. James Wardrop, the lettering scholar and Deputy Keeper of the Library (where he worked 1929–57) had from youth based his own hand on a Humanistic manuscript owned by Johnston and illustrated in this book. After Johnston's death in 1944, Wardrop was able to acquire it, and eventually his widow presented it to the Library.[13]

Johnston somewhat fulfilled the role to improve printed typography with a handful of type designs for private presses, but his widest impact on everyday lives was thanks to the remarkable Frank Pick, then commercial manager of London Transport, who commissioned him to design its typeface for signage, a version of which is still in use today. The V&A holds some examples from this project.

Like Cockerell, Wardrop was interested in contemporary calligraphy as well as its history; he developed the Library's collection of original work in the tradition Johnston so powerfully established through his remarkable penmanship and influential teaching (fig.15). Prominent in this line was Heather Child, represented in the Library by purchases and gifts of her own work and that of calligraphers internationally thanks to her influence.[14] Holdings were expanded with work from abroad, especially Germany, and by 1980 the Library was equipped to stage *The Universal Penman*, a major historical survey of lettering with a strong selection of contemporary work both British and foreign, including several new commissions.[15] The relationship of the writing arts to the real world was a theme of an associated book by the exhibition's curator, Joyce Irene Whalley. Important ceremonial uses for calligraphy and inscriptions persisted, sometimes of deep social significance, as in war memorial manuscripts and monuments. But Whalley also pointed out the proliferation of calligraphic text forms in commercial design, advertising and signage, as well as the importance for individuals of effective written literacy.[16]

As regards quotidian handwriting, Sydney Cockerell gave to the Library his collection of contemporary as well as historic

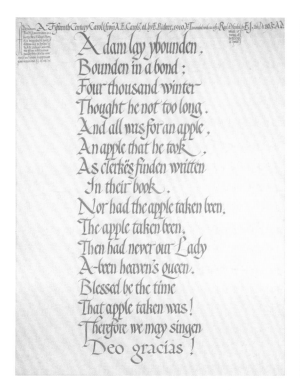

autograph letters from distinguished persons including
his own correspondents (Tolstoy, G.B. Shaw, William and
Jane Morris, Rupert Brooke, Henry James, Joseph Conrad, etc.)
as a corpus of examples.

One renowned graphic designer whose work grew from
a strong lettering foundation was the German Berthold Wolpe
(1905–1989): his influence on mainstream publishing design
in Britain was strong, through work for Stanley Morison at
the Monotype Corporation and a long career at Faber & Faber.
Wolpe was the subject of a retrospective exhibition staged
by the Library shortly after *The Universal Penman* exhibition
of 1980.[17]

In the later twentieth century, as with all the crafts, some
practitioners sought greater artistic autonomy with expressive
and experimental styles. A foremost example is Donald
Jackson, who has reinvented the scriptorium to create a new,
hand-written and illuminated Bible for the twenty-first century

(fig.16).[18] A selection of the plates was exhibited at the
V&A in 2006.

From the beginning, bindings were the parts of books
most prominently collected as objects in the Museum (see
p.32). (A statue of Roger Payne, the eighteenth-century master
of English binding, stands on the V&A's façade, at the right
hand of William Morris.) With the Re-arrangement of 1909,
'the bookbindings formerly exhibited in other departments
... have been with a few special exceptions incorporated with
the collection already in the Library'.[19] The Book Production
Gallery devoted a section to 'modern bookbindings', showing
both traditional workmanship and the modern influences
of Art Nouveau and the Arts and Crafts Movement.

Sarah Prideaux, one of the first women to have a professional
career in bookbinding and teaching, had an ongoing
relationship with the Library in the 1910s. As well as selling
and donating bindings and tools, she provided a course on

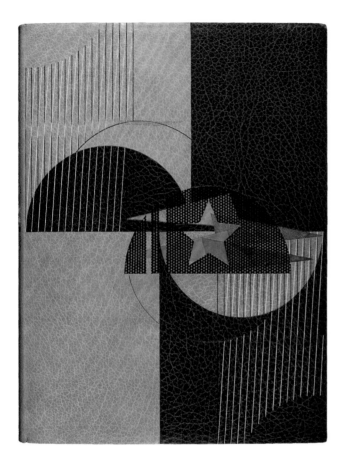

binding history in the form of lantern slides that could be circulated to art schools. Being also well versed in the history of engraving, she wrote a gallery guide for the technical displays on printing and binding mounted jointly by the Library and EID.[20]

In 1949 a major exhibition of bindings was held in the Library's gallery, including examples also from the independent collection made by 'Circulation', the department created to distribute loans and small displays to regional museums and art schools throughout the country. Since the Re-arrangement of 1909, 'Circ' had been able to build its own collections, which, like the Library's, were exempt from the 50-year rule, and as time went on 'The special requirements of Art Schools ... naturally led to an emphasis on contemporary work'.[21]

Circ staff were especially conversant with the current art world, and it was their Keeper, Peter Floud, who at this moment facilitated a series of commissions for the Library from some of the best French art binders to work on *livres d'artistes*, resulting in acquisitions from Rose Adler (fig.17) and Henri Creuzevault, and an iconic binding by Paul Bonet for Matisse's *Jazz*.[22]

This occasioned some remark among the British binding community, and a distinguished practitioner wrote to the Library proposing a British commission in like manner.[23] The Library did go on to acquire pieces from exhibitions of the Designer Bookbinders society, which formed from the mid-1950s. In 1971 an international touring exhibition of their work was shown at the V&A, and in 1978 there was a two-man display of William Matthews and Edgar Mansfield.[24]

This was a period of experiment and debate in binding, and British binders were at the forefront of what is referred to below as a 'new consciousness of the book'.[25] As with calligraphy, some binders sought to liberate or theorize their craft in the direction of independent art – in Britain notably Philip Smith,[26] from whom several major works were purchased.

The issues of relevance and sustainability of the craft were recognized in the Library: 'If hand binding is to survive in the modern world, enlightened patronage must ... play its part', wrote the Keeper in 1971.[27] A colleague later suggested that the 'quasi-silent echoes' of work distributed and consumed only in a single copy could be amplified through the influence of 'collectors of discrimination' – or by being copied for 'trade runs'.[28] Examples were acquired of trade books by French publishers such as Gallimard with covers by fine binding designers Paul Bonet and Mario Prassinos.

One way in which the Library, like others, supported bookbinders (especially under the Keeper Ronald Lightbown) was by commissioning conservation work from expert practitioners. Roger Powell, a veteran both in fine binding design and conservation, was entrusted with some of the most valuable manuscripts. More decorative bindings were provided

fig.18. David Sellars
binding for Charles Dickens,
The Mystery of Edwin Drood
(Clarendon Press, 1972)
West Yorkshire, 2012

to antiquarian printed books by distinguished binders including James Brockman, with spine decoration to enhance the look of the Library's reading rooms. More recently, in 1998 a creative commission was given to Eduardo Paolozzi – an artist and designer rather than a craft binder – to design a new binding for the 1934 Skira edition of Lautréamont's *Les chants de Maldoror* illustrated by Salvador Dalí, a volume that Paolozzi recalled consulting as a student in London in the 1940s (at which time it was clad in a sturdy, Government-issue buckram binding). The work was executed in collaboration between the artist, a Library curator and the V&A's book conservator. For its latest commission, on the occasion of the Charles Dickens Bicentenary in 2012, a top craftsman/designer binder was selected (fig.18).

New Approaches to Illustration

In 1935 the Library acquired the first two books published by Albert Skira (1904–1973), an edition of Ovid's *Metamorphoses* and the *Poésies* of Mallarmé, each with exquisite outline illustrations, by Picasso and Matisse respectively (figs 19, 20).

Skira was doing a special kind of art publishing, working with major artists to produce collectors' books of superb quality that matched either literary classics or contemporary poetry with original prints. Earlier examples had been set by French art dealers, especially Ambroise Vollard (see section 7 of the catalogue), but the field was stimulated in 1936 by a major exhibition at the Museum of Modern Art in New York;[29] many of the most famous works were produced during and after the Second World War.

LIVRE PREMIER

Je me propose de dire les métamorphoses des corps en des corps nouveaux; ô dieux, (car ces métamorphoses sont aussi votre ouvrage) secondez mon entreprise de votre souffle et conduisez sans interruption ce poème depuis les plus lointaines origines du monde jusqu'à mon temps.

7

LIVRE SIXIÈME

La déesse du Triton avait prêté l'oreille à ce récit; elle avait applaudi au chant des Aonides et à leur juste courroux. Alors elle se dit : « C'est peu de louer; méritons d'être louée aussi; ne permettons pas qu'on méprise impunément notre divinité. » Et elle songe à perdre la Méonienne Arachné, qui, lui avait-on dit, prétendait l'égaler dans l'art de tisser la laine. Celle-ci n'était célèbre ni par son rang ni par ses origines, elle ne l'était que par son art; son père, Idmon de Colophon, teignait avec la pourpre de Phocée

133

En vain! l'Azur triomphe, & je l'entends qui chante
Dans les cloches. Mon âme, il se fait voix pour plus
Nous faire peur avec sa victoire méchante,
Et du métal vivant sort en bleus angelus!

Il roule par la brume, ancien & traverse
Ta native agonie ainsi qu'un glaive sûr;
Où fuir dans la révolte inutile & perverse?
Je suis hanté. L'Azur! l'Azur! l'Azur! l'Azur!

42

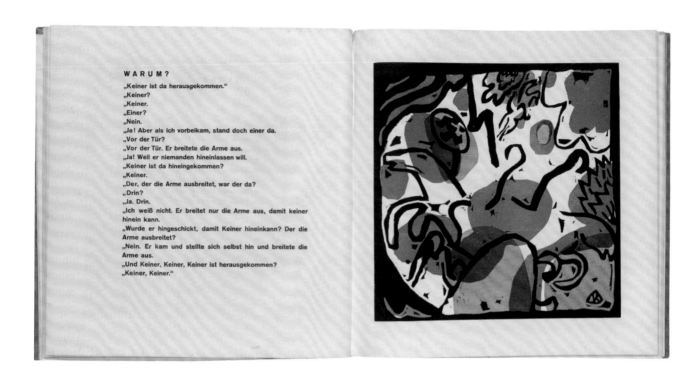

WARUM?

„Keiner ist da herausgekommen."
„Keiner?
„Keiner.
„Einer?
„Nein.
„Ja! Aber als ich vorbeikam, stand doch einer da.
„Vor der Tür?
„Vor der Tür. Er breitete die Arme aus.
„Ja! Weil er niemanden hineinlassen will.
„Keiner ist da hineingekommen?
„Keiner.
„Der, der die Arme ausbreitet, war der da?
„Drin?
„Ja. Drin.
„Ich weiß nicht. Er breitet nur die Arme aus, damit keiner
hinein kann.
„Wurde er hingeschickt, damit Keiner hineinkann? Der die
Arme ausbreitet?
„Nein. Er kam und stellte sich selbst hin und breitete die
Arme aus.
„Und Keiner, Keiner, Keiner ist herausgekommen?
„Keiner, Keiner."

fig.19. Pablo Picasso
Ovide: Les métamorphoses
(Lausanne: Skira, 1931)

fig.20. Henri Matisse, *Poésies de Stéphane*
Mallarmé (Lausanne: Skira, 1932)

fig.21. Wassily Kandinsky
Klänge (Munich: R. Piper, 1913)

In Germany, Reinhard Piper, Fritz Gurlitt and Kurt Wolff published similar books with Expressionist and Blaue Reiter artists (fig.21).

The Library's collection was greatly enhanced by a later gift (1996) of German Expressionist *livres d'artistes* collected by the art dealer Harry Fischer. Together with these books came a document of special historical importance: a copy of the detailed inventory compiled by the German Ministry of Propaganda of all works of art in German museums that were characterized as 'degenerate art', seized by the Nazi government and eventually sold off in 1941. The second half of this manuscript is a unique copy.

Both the creativity and the contemporary art-world connections within the Museum were manifested in a book of similar genre produced in 1940 for the Limited Editions Club by James Laver, then Assistant Keeper in EID. He compiled a collection of English translations of Baudelaire's *Fleurs du mal*, including one by his colleague Graham Reynolds and another by V&A Director Eric Maclagan. Expressionist-style images by Jacob Epstein were 'printed from the lithographic stone by Mourlot in Paris, in the year that France was occupied by the Nazi[s]'.[30] In 1948 the Library exhibited several such *livres d'artistes*, in a spirit of post-war affirmation, including Matisse's

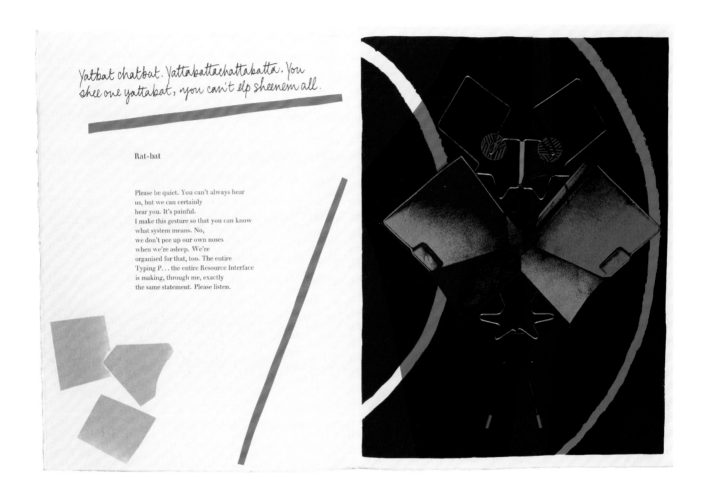

Jazz (Tériade, 1947), 'a book produced during the gravest months of the German Occupation'.[31]

These books were accessible to inspire artists and students in London who were exploring printmaking and book making in the 1950s and '60s. Print dealers and studio providers such as Alecto facilitated publishing for artists,[32] but the latter sometimes acted under their own imprint. The Circle Press, founded in 1967 by Ronald King, was a leading printmaker press for artists' illustrated books for at least 30 years: 'Matisse's *Jazz* moved me tremendously, a revelation'.[33] Likewise, Ian Tyson, who started the Tetrad Press in 1970, after working with King for a period, said:

The first time I remember the excitement of handling a book was at the Victoria and Albert Museum around 1966, when I asked to see Paul Eluard's *A toute épreuve* with its Miró woodcuts. It was a great privilege to be able to hold that: handling it was essential to the experience of the book. *A toute épreuve* changed something in my life.[34]

The Library aims to preserve its treasures for readers to enjoy in perpetuity, but allowing them full reading access has always been its ethos. Back in 1950, when Henri Creuzevault was commissioned to bind the Fabriani edition of Buffon's *Histoire naturelle* with Picasso's etchings (1942), 'he pointed out that many of the plates in the book were badly marked and rubbed'. Peter Floud 'explained that this was due to constant use by students over a period of four years.'[35] King and Tyson were doubtless inspired not only by the look and form of the de luxe books in the Library, but also by the quality of their literary texts: both artists chose to work with distinguished though non-mainstream poets.

Fifty years after the arrival of Skira's first books, the V&A's exhibition *From Manet to Hockney* (1985) showcased the Library's 'modern artists' illustrated books', including works by later generations, as well as by Americans. It was an exemplary selection of 167 items, from Mallarmé's and Manet's version of Poe's *Raven* (1875), to Richard Long's *Mud Hand Prints* (Coracle Press, 1984), including Surrealist and Expressionist books as well as some 'aesthetic' works of the 1890s that had been seen first in the inaugural displays of the Book Production Gallery.[36] Today, the Library continues very selectively to add new examples to its rich holdings showing the special quality notable artists bring to their encounter with the book (fig.23). In 2008 the exhibition *Blood on Paper* took a fresh look at the activity of major artists in the book format, with some spectacular loans in collaboration with Elena Ochoa Foster's Ivory Press (fig.33).

The Library encourages the regular trade side of publishing with annual Illustration Awards, inaugurated in 1972 thanks to a bequest from Francis Williams.[37] The first judges included book designer Ruari McLean, and David Hockney, whose own illustrative prints for Grimms' Fairy Tales formed a V&A travelling exhibition at the time. Books and magazines are judged for their internal illustrations or their cover or jacket. Prizewinning publications and other selected entrants are acquired for the Library, and today all entries, both professional and students', are archived online.

The rise of the book jacket in the twentieth century created a new opportunity for illustration and design, with a powerfully competitive purpose: the jacket exists not to enrich a text but purely to sell it. Jackets were collected as examples of graphic design, and in 1949 a pioneering exhibition of

book jackets from many countries was organized by Peter Floud, working with Charles Rosner, the editor of *The Studio* magazine's *Modern Publicity* supplements. Jackets continued to be actively collected for the Prints collection, while the Library took on responsibility for a large collection from the British Library of more than 500,000, with a view to their potential for large-scale interdisciplinary research.

The art of photography had increasingly provided popular circulating collections; when the Circulation Department was wound up in 1977, a curatorial collection of photographs was established within the Prints and Drawings Department. Though the Library's documentary collection of photographs was dispersed (see first chapter), the rise of the status of photography as art within the V&A and in the world at large

fig.24. Henri Cartier-Bresson
Images à la sauvette ['The decisive
moment'] (Paris: Editions Verve,
1952)

had the effect of creating a new art-bibliographical category, the photo book.[38] The Library naturally already held many important examples (fig.24); it continues to select from those that manifest a creative use of photography applied to the book format, whether by photographers of note who are represented also in the V&A's Photographs collection, or by artists who are not primarily known as photographers.

The visual and material requirements of children's books, especially in modern times, cause them to be seen as a separate category of book production, and they were displayed as such in 1909. In 1932 a major loan exhibition led to the bequest from Guy Little of 2,400 examples. Smaller donations followed (including a Soviet Russian group), but the arrival in 1970

of the Renier Collection of approximately 80,000 volumes gave the V&A the largest special collection of children's books in the country. The Reniers' intention in collecting had been to provide resources for social history, so this instance shows again how collections have changing meanings and uses.

The Art of Distribution: Avant-Garde Art and Corporate Publicity

Fine illustrated books containing original prints, complex and expensive to produce, are rarely the initiative of an artist.[39] Artists, however, have often felt impelled to publish, and during the course of the twentieth century a series of avant-garde art movements was characterized by books

by visual or literary artists, often in collaboration. Most of these were not expensive productions but made according to normal trade standards, commonly self-published or supported by a publisher or gallerist who facilitated rather than directed. These are more definitely *artists*' books, a consequence of the urge not only to express but also to distribute their work, message or ideas. In some cases intended first and foremost to reach like-minded activists, books such as these could take some time to arrive in the Library collections.

Launched by the poet F.T. Marinetti in 1909, Futurism was the first of these movements to produce exhilarating, consciously revolutionary pamphlets, books and magazines, finding innovative ways to turn the constraints of cheap

formats to their advantage. The Library received the catalogue of the exhibition that Marinetti brought to London in 1912,[40] and caught up with Futurist publications later in the 1930s, together with Wyndham Lewis's Vorticist *Blast* (1913–14) and the international Dada publications of the 1920s (fig.25).

Russian Futurist books were among acquisitions from Mikhail Larionov and Natalia Goncharova, artist-designers associated with the Ballets Russes, thanks to Brian Reade, Deputy Keeper of Prints and Drawings, when in 1961 he visited their Paris home to purchase original theatre and costume designs. The books selected included works by the poets Aleksei Kruchenykh and Velimir Khlebnikov, exponents of *zaum*, or 'transrational' writing, with semi-invented

Within the image:

Le Vin contre la
Dépression Nerveuse
et l'Anémie

6

"Le Vin est le remède héroïque de ce que"
"Bouchardat appelait la misère physiologique,"
"c'est-à-dire la dépression, le dépérissement."
DOCTEUR F. DOUGNAC

Et il cite le cas d'un américain adepte du régime sec,
fatigué, neurasthénique, guéri par le Saint-Émilion. Il
précise enfin que le vin contient du fer, du phosphore,
et bien d'autres éléments que nous ne connaissons pas,
sous une forme vivante et parfaitement assimilable,
des diastases, des vitamines et des corps radio-actifs.

"Le vin, lorsqu'il est pris en quantités raison-"
"nables, retentit toujours utilement aussi bien"
"sur le moral que sur l'activité et la puissance de"
"production des muscles." DOCTEUR J. ALQUIER

"Les affections nerveuses sans substratum"
"organique, celles surtout reconnaissant une"
"étiologie toute morale, la nostalgie, l'hypocondrie, indiquent sur-"
"tout l'emploi du vin." DOCTEUR FONSSAGRIVES
"Les anémiques, les chlorotiques, les convalescents ne peuvent se"
"passer de vin." DOCTEUR PETON

fig.26. Raoul Dufy
illustrations in Gaston Derys,
Mon docteur le vin (Paris: Draeger
Frères, 1936)

vocabulary, as well as Igor Terentiev's rare *Tract of Total Indecency* (Tbilisi, 1920).

A central aspect of these movements was the 'liberation' of language, for instance, by reproducing text directly from the author's handwriting by lithography, or by using the full resources of available commercial typography for expressive purposes, composed across the page in all sizes and styles. In the National Art Library, where the arts of the word – lettering and typography – have been collected for the purpose of informing and furthering good design, these works have a special relevance. In this context, their assertion of visible text as a medium of artistic expression not only contests rationalist design conventions and taste but can also deepen our approach to historic styles and their meanings. The appearance and techniques of avant-garde art typography, too, derived from the clamorous impact of modern publicity. The impact was registered in art when Picasso and Braque introduced newspaper mastheads and fragments of display text into their Cubist paintings, while Marinetti's whole project was based on publicity campaigns, with manifestos published in newspapers and leaflets distributed in the street.

The Library and the Prints collections early recognized the artistic quality and vocational relevance of what they catalogued as 'Advertisement art' in poster acquisitions. In Britain, following Germany and the United States, the expansion of this field of opportunities for artists and ancillary professionals was reflected in new organizations, trade exhibitions and publications available in the Library. *The Studio* magazine, which had championed the new styles at the turn of the nineteenth century, started a new title, *Commercial Art*, in 1922, with its own supplements on posters and 'modern publicity', for example. The Jobbing Printing collection of 'modern commercial typography' was begun in 1936, when material was solicited directly from leading international design firms and their clients (see section 5 of the catalogue). It is valuable as an assemblage of its era, drawn on today for both creative inspiration and historical research.[41] Among other things, the collection evidences the breadth and quality of work done in commercial graphics by fine artists (fig.26).[42]

A local version of the Jobbing Printing collecting initiative is the annual 'High Street Trawl', initiated at the Archive of Art and Design in 1986. Curators go out annually on 16 June to collect examples of printed ephemera from everyday contexts. Economical of time, storage and documentation, the collection is expected to capture sociological as much as typographic glimpses of London through time, and is gradually acquiring critical mass and historical value. The collecting day is of course 'Bloomsday', in homage to James Joyce's *Ulysses* and his intense absorption in the visual and material quiddity of location – and treatment of items such as newspapers and the 'Elijah' pamphlet, thrown in the river but recurring to view.[43]

Just as the V&A librarians were assembling printed ephemera from the likes of Herbert Bayer, Swiss Federal Railways and the BBC, a former V&A curator, Herbert Read, was occupied in helping to organize the International Surrealist Exhibition in London (1936). 'Do not judge this movement kindly. It is not just another amusing stunt. It is . . . the desperate act of men . . . profoundly convinced of the rottenness of our civilization,' declared Read in the catalogue.[44] Nonetheless, like the earlier distinctive styles of Art Nouveau and Art Deco, Surrealism was a powerful influence on mainstream marketing graphics, for instance in the work of Hans Schleger, 'Zero'. Examples were collected from his firm in the 1936 survey; his large archive was eventually donated in 1995.

Unlike many of their contemporaries, Surrealist-affiliated artists such as Magritte and Man Ray disparaged the commercial illustration to which they resorted for economic reasons. Max Ernst's collages, however, were specifically inspired by a 'hallucinatory' moment of response to an illustrated trade catalogue. At all events, some of the publications that the Surrealists undertook themselves remain among the most exciting artists' books ever conceived, through the force of their texts and images, even though in material terms they are relatively conventional and they eschew the visually experimental text that characterized Dada publications. Surrealism used innovative methods to evade intentionality and release unconscious motifs; book projects suggested collaborations that could divert even further from premeditation. Furthermore, the privacy of the book is apt to deliver a more absorbing and intimately disquieting experience to the reader than a large painting.

In the 1930s the Library acquired a good representation of publications by (and about) Surrealists and other advanced artists. Like most other illustrated books, they were not segregated into 'special collections', but made available without restriction to readers, protected if necessary with standard library bindings. The catalogue of the Paris Surrealist exhibition of 1947 was acquired in the special version, with Marcel Duchamp's designed cover b(e)aring an imitation rubber breast ('Prière de toucher'), for the Bindings collection.

fig.27. Helene Fesenmaier
Log Book, text by Hildebrand
von Heldesheym, calligraphy
by Eileen Hogan (London, 1979)
Commissioned for *The Open
and Closed Book* exhibition

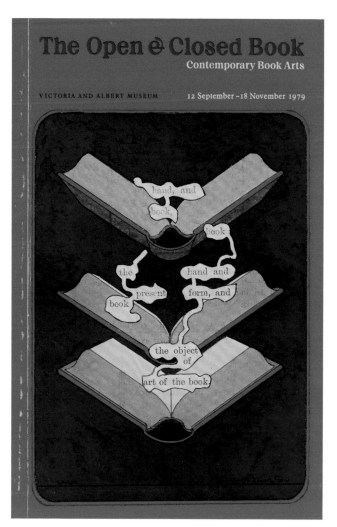

fig.28. *The Open and Closed Book:*
Contemporary Book Arts
(London: Victoria and Albert
Museum, 1979)
Cover illustration by Tom Phillips

A New Consciousness of the Book

In 1979 the V&A mounted *The Open and Closed Book*, a large
exhibition of 'contemporary book arts', mainly but not
exclusively British, and with a very wide range of aspects:
'Private presses, Illustration, Fine binding, Concrete poetry,
Typography, Conceptual art, Commercial publishers,
Children's books, Calendars, Ex-libris designs, Literature,
Models, maquettes (three-dimensional objects), Audio-visual
aids'.[45] It was curated by R.C. (Robert) Kenedy (1926–1980),
a creative and original Hungarian who had settled in Britain
after the Second World War and became a librarian, joining
the V&A in 1963 thanks to encouragement from the Director,
Trenchard Cox, whom he had supposedly met through a
chance encounter in the street.[46] Kenedy was a writer, teacher
and poet, and an advisory editor and frequent reviewer on *Art
International* magazine. After his untimely death, the American
critic Lucy Lippard called him a 'Friend to artists . . . intellectual
maverick . . . a civilized man'.[47] It was the direct involvement
of many artists and publishers, advising, lending work, and in
some cases making new work, especially, that enabled Kenedy
to put together this remarkably wide-ranging exhibition of
contemporary publications and related material.[48]

    The Open and Closed Book juxtaposed art-orientated aspects
of publishing – both de luxe and cheap – with a focus on
high quality in the contemporary everyday. The 'Illustration'
section ranged from fine art prints to Monty Python designs
by Terry Gilliam and cartoon books by Norman Thelwell;
the Typography section was devoted to founts for photo
typesetting;[49] a large section showed books from 'Commercial
publishers', with particular reference to paperback cover
design and children's books (fig.28).

    Some categories in this conspectus of 'book arts' were
unheard of when the scope of 'book production' was
defined for the Library in 1909 (see p.46). The first of
these was concrete poetry, although Kenedy asserted its
continuity with a core lettering tradition: 'Concrete poetry
is directly related to Renaissance epigraphy'.[50] He had
already championed the work of Ian Hamilton Finlay, the

pre-eminent Scottish artist associated with concrete poetry,
for whom inscription indeed was a central activity,[51] and
received 'a steady stream . . . of information, encouragement
and practical advice' from him while preparing *The Open and
Closed Book*.[52] Kenedy was also delighted to achieve for Finlay
– and likewise Tom Phillips – commissions for bookplates to
be sold at the Museum: 'these four compositions represent
the V&A's active participation in the exhibition'.[53] A new
typeface was also commissioned.[54]

fig.29. Dom sylvester houédard
'Typestract': 'Cultic textsite
excavated at Rasshamra'
England(?), 1969

fig.30. Simon Cutts
'Poinsettia', name-tapes
(London: Coracle, 1975[?])

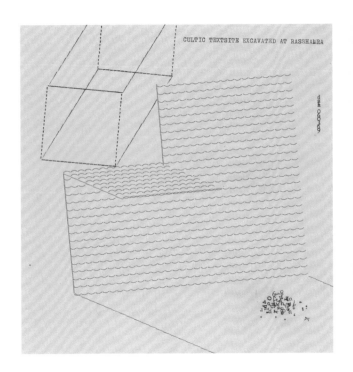

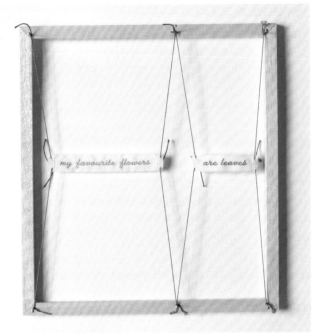

Concrete poetry is sometimes thought synonymous with 'pattern poetry' and Futurist wildness, but uniform sans-serif faces in standard verse layouts were as typical of it as shaped or spatially extended typography. The brevity and speed of contemporary demotic and mass-media graphics were as influential as a spectacular or sculptural approach to language, according to Eugen Gomringer, a founding father of the movement, in 1954: 'abbreviated restricted forms of language are emerging ... restriction in the best sense – concentration and simplification – is the very essence of poetry ... Headlines, slogans, groups of sounds and letters give rise to forms which could be models for a new poetry'.[55]

Another factor was the availability to poets and small press editors of typesetting technologies, so that text design could become part of authorship. The typewriter became a creative tool for many, including the Guernsey-born Benedictine monk Dom sylvester houédard (1924–1992).[56] A circulating collection of his 'typestracts' was made by the V&A in 1971 (fig.29).[57]

The same could apply to the means of print production: 'The fairly severe limitations of the Adana have been a continuing influence on my poetry,'[58] wrote Thomas A. Clark, whose Moschatel Press from 1973 published small pamphlets and cards 'designed for the mantelpiece rather than the bookshelf'.[59]

The most substantial investment in this field of poetry publishing as an art practice was the purchase in 1990 of a complete file of publications from the Coracle Press. Coracle was founded in 1975 by the poet Simon Cutts, later joined by American artist Erica Van Horn, initially in conjunction with an art gallery. As with Finlay, there was an openness to whatever physical form seemed right for an idea, as well as the migration of some ideas from one form to another (fig.30). Some publications resembled artists' multiples rather than books; others were deliberately ephemeral.[60]

Affordable commercial printing lay behind the artists' books associated with Conceptual Art in the 1960s. The American artist Edward Ruscha's deadpan photographic

fig.31. Helen Douglas and Telfer Stokes
Chinese Whispers
(London: Weproductions, 1976)

sequences from the early 1960s are considered the first of their kind.[61] Kenedy's selection provided a view of the distinctive flavours of British conceptual photo books, their motifs often non-urban-landscape-based (Richard Long, Hamish Fulton), explicitly socio-political (Victor Burgin, Stephen Willats) or serio-comic (Gilbert & George, John Stezaker).[62] A strong response to Ruscha's books was that of Telfer Stokes, who in the early 1970s evolved a mode admitting rhythm, lyricism and visual narrative (fig.31).

One new term that did not appear in *The Open and Closed Book*, despite having gained recent currency in the art world, was 'artist's book',[63] resulting in occasionally contrived classifications,[64] but avoiding the difficulties of definition.[65] Critical commentary around a field named 'artists' books' began to emerge in the 1980s,[66] shortly before the arrival of Jan van der Wateren, a Keeper keen to build up this collection.[67] Funding in that era was still generous, and by the mid-1990s the Library could claim to have the foremost collection of artists' books, of all kinds, in Britain. In the art and design museum context, some works were welcomed that other libraries ruled out of scope, including unique books and sculptural objects (fig.32). (A few such objects had been included in Kenedy's section of 'Models, maquettes and three-dimensional objects', including the 14-foot [4.3-m] wooden book sculpture installed on the pavement outside the main entrance of the V&A – see fig.27).

More work by individual artists whose chief focus was the book was now acquired: Ken Campbell, Timothy Ely, Gloria Helfgott, Ulrike Stoltz, Mikhail Karasik and numerous others. Subscriptions were committed to selected projects, such as Claire Van Vliet's Janus Press (founded in Vermont in 1955), books based on precise paper and book crafts; the annual assembled miscellanies of Field Study International (from 1995); and the decade-long, 50-volume *Zweite Enzyklopädie von Tlön* (1997–2006) by Peter Malutzki and Ines von Ketelhodt. By the turn of the twentieth century the resource had reached a critical mass and collecting became more selective. It is very well used, especially by art and design students.

fig.32. Geneviève Seillé
Mapa ed Veneiis,
Burton on Trent, 1990

Jan van der Wateren was equally committed to comics, the mass-market 'word and image' genre par excellence, which in the 1990s also started to attract academic attention. Several large collections were acquired, building substantially on existing holdings that go back to nineteenth-century illustrated proto-comic works by Rodolphe Töpffer and Wilhelm Busch. Modern comics in large numbers are found in the Renier Collection, and are a major focus of the 'Krazy Kat Arkive', Eduardo Paolozzi's collection of popular culture (fig.34).

As the digital age progresses, the Library continues both to document and to collect the activity of artists in publications. Their enthusiasm for print seems as yet undiminished, with digital media used to originate, enhance, supplement, distribute and promote their work, rather than ultimately to dematerialize it. A noteworthy acquisition is the Archizines collection of fanzines produced by young architects internationally.[68] An example of a digital supplement is the app for Tom Phillips's well-known *Humument*, with its unique 'oracle' feature (fig.35).

Convergences

This essay has briefly highlighted the main aspects of the National Art Library's curatorial collecting since the early twentieth century. As a public reference library supporting studies in art and design, however, most of its acquisitions are made as information sources rather than as examples of the book arts. To give a properly rounded view, the pithy collecting statement of 1911 can be revisited in a little more detail:

fig.33. *Blood on Paper* exhibition,
2008, showing Damien Hirst's 'New
Religion' and 'Francis Bacon: Detritus',
facsimiles by Ivory Press

fig.34. Objects and publications in
the Krazy Kat Arkive of Twentieth
Century Popular Culture, collected
and given by Eduardo Paolozzi

'The principal aim of the Library is the acquisition, for the use of readers, of the more important new books on fine and applied art, produced in this country or abroad'.[69]

While the subject scope – 'fine and applied art' – was comprehensive, the coverage has been selective: only 'the more important' works. The ideal of comprehensiveness persisted as funding both rose and fell over the following century, but the growth of publishing obviously outstripped any hope of keeping up.[70] Today, when the focus of 'art' itself has widened greatly and the challenge of appropriate selectivity increased, the aim is to sharpen a documentary collection that fulfils the Library's character as part of the V&A and contributes distinctively to national and international information networks. The ability to track down almost any work required, somewhere in the world, with the growing hope of obtaining it in full-text electronic form, truly fulfils the aspiration of the 'universal catalogue'.

As in most disciplines, the term 'books' covers a number of genres and formats. In the arts, catalogues of various kinds are of course crucial. Private and royal collection catalogues have been especially prized.[71] Catalogues of fine and decorative art sales, containing valuable and otherwise fugitive information about individual objects, have also been acquired primarily by

deposit from the leading auction houses. Since the Library was surveyed by Frits Lugt for his *Répertoire des catalogues de ventes publiques* (1938–87), no other library in Britain has collected and individually catalogued these on so large a scale.

Relationships and exchange agreements with numerous institutions worldwide helped to create a collection of exhibition catalogues that could hardly have been matched in any other way. Further, since 1996 the National Art Library has supported the British Library's role, by housing and cataloguing the smaller art exhibition catalogues received through legal deposit.

The trade catalogues and related ephemera that are rich sources of information about designed goods, their creation, markets and use, and of which the Library has numerous historic holdings, through both retrospective and contemporaneous acquisition, are mentioned in the previous essay. A renewed collecting programme was initiated in the early 1990s, soliciting ongoing donations from selected leading design and retail firms.

The Library has the leading British collection of international art and design periodicals.[72] Under the aegis of the art libraries society ARLIS UK & Ireland, these holdings formed the basis of a union catalogue for the nation's art

fig.35. Tom Phillips (b.1937)
A Humument
App 2012

libraries, before the advent of large-scale electronic network providers.[73]

In 1976 an exhibition, *The Art Press: Two Centuries of Art Magazines*, was staged, and also an international conference in collaboration with ARLIS. The proceedings were a real contribution to art historiography, referring not only to magazine illustration and design – and artists' own forays into serial publishing (fig.36) – but also exploring the origins of connoisseurial and scholarly art periodicals, their impact on the lineaments of the subject, and their possible future in light of economic and technological changes.[74] Taken together, the papers' perspectives transcend the binary division between 'the art of the book' and publications considered purely as conduits of information.

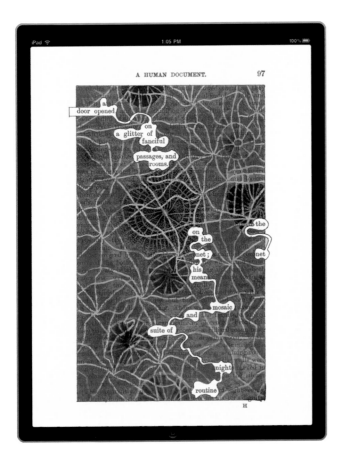

A similar viewpoint was articulated more recently in a case study of catalogues and publications through which the 'Young British Artists' were promoted in the 1990s.[75] At around the same time the National Art Library began to contribute to new Book History degree courses for the University of London.[76] Library management is a pragmatic science, but intrinsic to the Library that is part of an art and design museum is the understanding that information is material, that the text and image resources provided for study and research are themselves artefacts, worthy of study.

Similar reflections were aroused by a display in 1995, *The Book and Beyond: Electronic Publishing and the Art of the Book.*[77] As a librarian, its curator was well aware of the difference made to research and to information services, not least in the National Art Library itself, by 'computerization' over the preceding two decades, but this display registered the moment in the mid-1990s when the potential of digital media had begun to be exploited successfully not only by commercial and cultural publishers but also by creative artists. Thus recently acquired artists' books were juxtaposed with informational and documentary resources, delivered by programs such as Apple's Hypercard and on physical carriers including floppy disks and videodiscs, by now largely archaic.[78] A notable inclusion was *Agrippa: A Book of the Dead*, an artists' book combining delicate etchings with a utilitarian floppy disk containing a text, by William Gibson – doyen of information-age science fiction – that would supposedly erase itself after one reading on a computer.[79]

One implication of this relatively modest but acute and timely display was followed up in the Word and Image Department, primarily through the formation of a Computer Art collection.[80] In the Library, computers continued for the most part to dispense information. Meanwhile, out in the world, computerization was followed by 'digitization' – the creation of digital surrogates for books of all kinds – a topic too large and complex to address here, save to note one happy outcome for the librarian/curator: a book can be put on display and still remain available for reading. Not either/or: both.

fig.36. Alfred Stieglitz (ed.)
291 (New York: Gallery 291, 1915),
nos 5 and 6
Cover portrait of Stieglitz
by Francis Picabia

Art, Books and Design
from the National Art Library

The opening of the new museum established after the Great
Exhibition of 1851 prompted the publication of a number
of glamorous de luxe books by the leaders of design reform.
The books, which celebrated the Museum's educational role
and philosophy, used the latest advances in printing and
photography. Their images in colour were hailed as technological
marvels. Two of these publications (Digby Wyatt's *Industrial
Arts* of 1851–3 and Waring's *Masterpieces of Industrial Art* of 1863)
showed objects of exemplary good taste and design from the
world's International Exhibitions of 1851 and 1862. They were
among books circulated to regional art schools by the Museum's
library. Another of them, the *Treasury of Ornamental Art* (1857)
with texts by J.C. Robinson, gave an account of objects that
had been selected for the new museum; use of photography
gave the images unprecedented accuracy. Most important for
teaching was Owen Jones's *Grammar of Ornament* of 1856,
which analysed the ornament of all known human societies:
human communities could be understood best by the study
of their ornament, and the Museum's collections would provide
evidence. All these books trumpeted the message that design
and art could be harnessed to industry to create works that
satisfied every demand of taste and utility.

GROUP OF GLASS, BY COUNT HARRACH OF BOHEMIA

LONDON, PRINTED AND PUBLISHED FEBY 15TH 1852 BY DAY & SON, LITHOGRAPHERS TO THE QUEEN.

2

Egyptian ornament, artwork by Owen Jones (1809–1874) for plates in his *Grammar of Ornament... Illustrated from Various Styles... Drawn on Stone by Francis Bedford* (London: Day & Son, 1856)

The Library acquired multiple copies of the published version of this work to circulate to provincial art schools. Architectural students were drilled in ornament: this artwork was first stored in the architectural museum, where Jones's earlier publication of the ornament at the Alhambra Palace in Granada was available.

1 (PREVIOUS PAGE)

Glass vessels by Count Harrach of Bohemia, plate 38 from Matthew Digby Wyatt (1820–1877), *The Industrial Arts of the Nineteenth Century: A Series of Illustrations of the Choicest Specimens... at the Great Exhibition of the Works of Industry, 1851* (London: Day & Son, 1851–3)

The glass came from the factory of Count Harrach in Bohemia, an enterprise set up in the eighteenth century.

3 (OPPOSITE)

Quiver and Indian fan,
plate 47 from J.C. Robinson
(1824–1913), *The Treasury of
Ornamental Art: Illustrations of Objects
of Art and Vertù Photographed and
Drawn on Stone by Francis Bedford*
(London: Day & Son, 1857)

The quiver and fan were made at
Jodhpur, with raised embroidery
of gold thread on blue velvet. They
were said to have 'all the usual taste
and decorative propriety of Hindoo
textile ornamentation'.

4

Pistols from Liège and London,
plate 95 from John Burley Waring
(1823–1875), *Masterpieces of
Industrial Art and Sculpture
at the International Exhibition,
Chromolithographed by ... W.R. Tymms,
A. Warren and G. Macculloch, from
Photographs ... Taken ... by Stephen
Thompson* (London: Day & Son, 1863)

The pistols include three revolvers,
made by R. Adams and E.M. Reilly
of London and Bayer Bros of Liège,
on the design that 'Colonel Colt
perfected after discovering the idea
from 17th-century Italian models'.

I
Resources for Art and Design Education

The notion that 'Design' was different from fine art was central to the beliefs of those arguing for a new kind of art training. William Dyce (1806–1864), in charge of the Government School of Design from 1837 to 1843, proposed a separate curriculum for 'ornamentists': they were to be drilled in mechanical drawing exercises while the fine artists were to study the works of great masters. But he agreed, grudgingly, that both should share some element of training, and the library of the Government School and of the new museum testifies to this common agenda. The Library, in fact, ensured that future designers had systematic exposure to fine art. Henry Townsend (1810–1890), Master and later Superintendent of the Government Schools of Design, noted that it was 'a great pity that any difference should be made between the instruction given to any person who is to be an ornamentist and that given to a pure artist'.

Whatever the theoretical debates, the Library sought from the outset to provide resources that enabled any kind of artist to make a living, whether engaged in ornamental, figurative, topographical or scientific work. The Library documented the human and natural world in an encyclopedic way, providing students with works that were factually correct and authoritative. Students would go on to work in an environment where the accurate knowledge of natural forms, historic and contemporary styles of furniture, portraiture, costume and architecture, for example, was essential to satisfy clients. As the antiquary and scholar Samuel Rush Meyrick (1783–1848) remarked, 'an anachronism in an historical picture is as offensive to the eye of taste as an imperfect metaphor or a defective verse to the ear' (quoting Henry Shaw's prospectus in the introduction to Shaw's *Specimens of Ancient Furniture*, 1836, p.2). Despite political undercurrents that pitted partisans of Gothic styles against supporters of classical Grecian purity or Baroque splendour, the Library collected works on these and other styles in abundance from its earliest days.

Study of the natural world was fundamental, and the 'General principles of Instruction' for the students at the Government School and the new museum's Art Library specifically included the drawing of flowers, foliage and objects of natural history from copies, as well as studies that treated natural objects ornamentally. Books on natural history, with their collections of botanical, geological and zoological illustrations, represented a significant part of the acquisitions made during the early decades of the Library. Townsend found that students 'constantly mention the works on Botany, containing plates of flowers, as among the most useful in the lending library'. By the mid-1860s there were scientific works, like Robert Thornton's exposition of Linnaeus's work on the reproduction of plants (*New Illustration of the Sexual System of Carolus von Linnaeus*, 1799–1810), as well as the beautifully illustrated work on lilies by Pierre-Joseph Redouté in the Didot edition of 1802–16. These were joined after Chauncy Hare Townshend's gift of 1868 by Audubon's *The Birds of America* (London, 1827–38), and the 11 volumes of the second edition of Buffon's *Histoire naturelle* (Paris, 1750–64), perhaps the most influential of the works produced by scientific thought of the eighteenth-century Enlightenment.

5
'Lokje-lockje', i.e. Banded Mantis Shrimp (*Lysiosquilla maculate*) and the fish called 'Passer: Le filou' [Passer: The trickster], i.e. Sling-jaw Wrasse (*Epibulus insidiator*), by Samuel Fallours, in Louis Renard (*c.*1678–1746), *Poissons, écrevisses, et crabes ... que l'on trouve autour des Isles Moluques et sur les Côtes des terres australes*, 2nd edn (Amsterdam: Ottens, 1754), vol. 1, fol. 42

Bequeathed by the Revd Chauncy Hare Townshend 1868

The prints, coloured by hand, were based on drawings by Samuel Fallours, an ex-soldier who lived on the island of Ambon, Indonesia. Details of the shrimp and wrasse are here broadly accurate, but many creatures recorded in this book were exaggerated or invented to satisfy western taste for exotica.

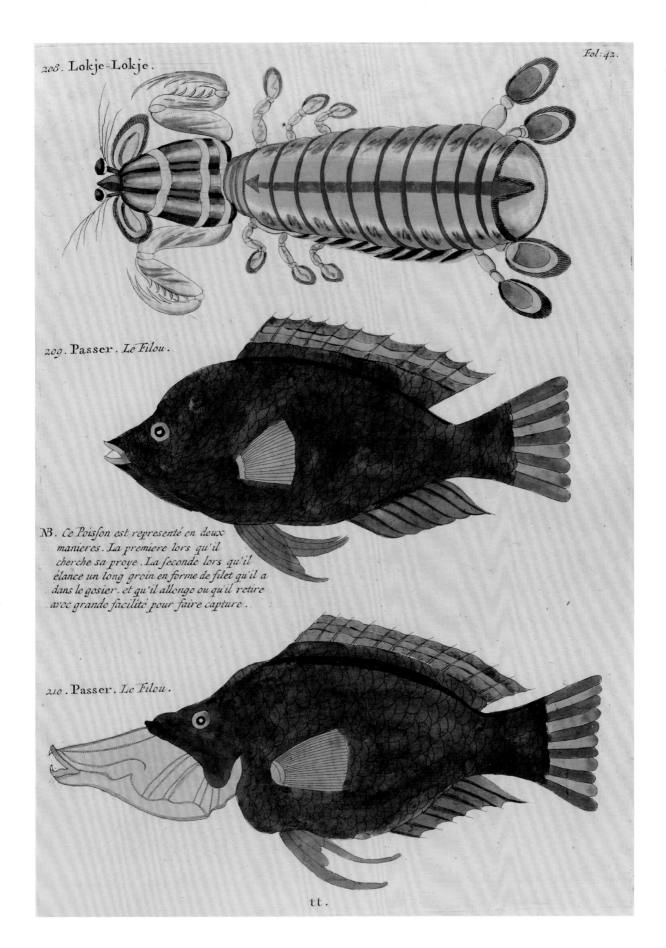

208. Lokje-Lokje.

Fol:42.

209. Passer. Le Filou.

NB. Ce Poisson est representé en deux
manieres. La premiere lors qu'il
cherche sa proye. La seconde lors qu'il
élance un long groin en forme de filet qu'il a
dans le gosier. et qu'il allonge ou qu'il retire
avec grande facilité pour faire capture..

210. Passer. Le Filou.

tt.

6
Dodo, Dragonfly and Dromedary,
plate XLI in 'William Frederic
Martyn' (i.e. William Fordyce Mavor,
1758–1837), *A New Dictionary of
Natural History; or, Compleat Universal
Display of Animated Nature ... Elegantly
Coloured* (London: Harrison & Co.,
1785), vol. 1
Hand-coloured engraving

Copying 'flat' depictions of the
animals was included in course
instructions for the School of
Design in the 1840s. Animals here
are described alphabetically. The
dictionary is based on the collection
of the Leverian Museum, a natural
history collection displayed to the
public in London from 1775.

7 (OPPOSITE)
**'Macrocercus Aracanga, Red &
Yellow Maccaw'** by Edward Lear
(1812–1888), plate 7 in *Illustrations
of the Family of Psittacidae or Parrots ...
Drawn from Life and on Stone*
(London: E. Lear, 1832)

Lear, before the publication of his
famous nonsense poems, was an
outstanding zoological illustrator.
When aged 18, he began a two-year
stint drawing in the Parrot House
at Regent's Park (London Zoo).
The images were lithographed
and then coloured by hand.

MACROCERCUS ARACANGA.

Red and Yellow Maccaw.

2/3 Nat. Size.

The admirable Butterfly

A.M. 3267.ᵃ '56.   demongues.   V.A.M.

8 (OPPOSITE)
Wild daffodil and Red Admiral butterfly, by Jacques Le Moyne De Morgues (*c.*1533–1588), France, *c.*1575
Watercolour and bodycolour on paper

Le Moyne's set of 59 botanical paintings combine acutely observed drawing with the clarity and stylization of an illustrated herbal. They were contained in a superb 16th-century French binding, of a kind collected by the Library as models for students. In the 1920s the paintings were removed to the Prints and Drawings Department, the binding remaining in the Library.

9
Binding, done in France, *c.*1575, for the Jacques Le Moyne De Morgues album (see previous)

Historic bindings were collected as examples of applied ornament.

10
Foliage cluster with Morning Glory, in Mary Gartside (active 1781–1809), *Ornamental Groups, Descriptive of Flowers, Birds, Fruit, Insects Etc. and Illustrative of a New Theory of Colouring* (London: W. Miller, 1808)
Hand-coloured lithographic print

As well as a botanical artist, Mary Gartside was a pioneer of colour theory. This album was produced as an instructional book for amateur artists. The list of subscribers, mostly female, is headed by the wife of George III, Queen Charlotte (1744–1818), who studied both botany and botanical illustration.

BILLY WATERS.

TYROL
Passeyer.

11
'Billy Waters, The Dancing Fiddler',
by Thomas, Lord Busby (1754–1838),
in *Costume of the Lower Orders of London*
(London: Published for T.L. Busby by
Messrs Baldwin, Cradock and Joy, 1820)
Hand-coloured etching

Thomas Busby introduces his
work hoping 'that students in rustic
picturesque character will find
the costumes proper subjects for
copying'. Billy Waters (1778–1823)
was an itinerant London musician
who became a celebrity. As a one-
legged ex-sailor from America, he
supported his family by 'Fiddling,
Dancing & Singing'.

12
'Tyrol, Passeyer', plate 72 in Albert
Kretchmer (1825–1891), *Deutsche
Volkstrachten* [German folk costumes],
vol. 2 (Leipzig: J.G. Bach, 1870)
Chromolithographic print

Kretchmer was a costumier to
the Royal Court Theatre in Berlin.
He recorded local traditions of dress
in German provinces. After the
Napoleonic wars, antiquarians in
many European states examined
traditional costume in great detail,
seen today as part of efforts to
reinforce national identities.

13 (OPPOSITE)
'Nesouaquoit: A Fox Chief',
by Charles Bird King (1785–1862),
in Thomas McKenney (1785–1859)
and James Hall (1793–1868), *History
of the Indian Tribes of North America*
(Philadelphia: E. Biddle, 1836),
vol. 1, p.154 verso
Hand-coloured lithographic print

Charles King painted the leaders of
at least 20 tribes, and also scenes
of Indian life. The original portraits,
gathered by McKenney for the War
Department in Washington DC,
were destroyed by fire. Nesouaquoit
wears a portrait medallion around
his neck, possibly a diplomatic gift,
with an image of Andrew Jackson,
President of the United States from
1829 to 1837.

NE-SOU-A QUOIT

A FOX CHIEF

Philadelphia Published by F.C.Biddle

Entered according to act of Congress in the year 1837 by F.C. Biddle in the Clerks office of the District Court of the Eastern District of P[?]

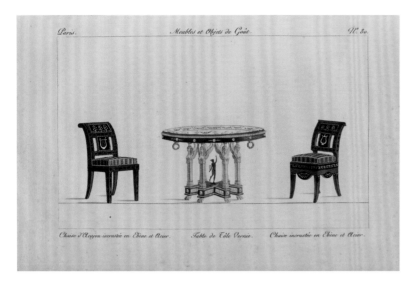

14
Table and two chairs, plate 80 in
Pierre de la Mésangère (1761–1831),
*Collection de meubles et objets de goût,
comprenant tout ce qui a rapport à
l'ameublement, tel que vases, tripieds,
candelabres, canalettes* (Paris, 1801–35)

These plates are from a volume of
engravings taken from the *Journal
des dames et des modes* (1802–35).
This collection included designs in
contemporary styles; de la Mésangère
used new, fashionable terminology
to describe the furniture.

15
State drawing room, plate 152 in
George Smith, *A Collection of Designs for
Household Furniture and Interior Decoration,
in the Most Approved and Elegant Taste . . .*
(London: J. Taylor, 1808)

George Smith emphasizes the
importance of architectural principles
in achieving grandeur and elegance.
In this design he uses columns standing
on plinths of equal height to the sofas
and chairs accommodated within
the recesses between the pillars. In this
way 'the view of the architecture is
preserved entire'.

16
Couch from Penshurst Place,
plate 5 in *Specimens of Ancient Furniture,
Drawn from Existing Authorities
by Henry Shaw FSA with Descriptions
by Sir Samuel Rush Meyrick* (London:
William Pickering, 1836)

The antiquarian and scholar Henry
Shaw (1800–1873) provided a series
of facsimiles of medieval and later
artefacts that were published in colour
by William Pickering. They provided
accurate models for painters. Shaw
attributes the couch to the reign of
William III (1689–1702).

17 (OPPOSITE)
Bed, plate 23 in *Furniture with Candelabra
and Interior Decorations Designed by R.
Bridgens* (London: William Pickering, 1838)

This bed was designed by Richard Bridgens
in the Grecian style. This publication,
with designs in Grecian, Elizabethan and
Gothic styles, provided a major source
for historicist Victorian design. Earlier in
his career Bridgens had provided designs
for the furnishings of Abbotsford House,
home of Sir Walter Scott.

Designed and Etched by R.Bridgens.

18 (ABOVE)

'Plan et coupe d'une partie de l'intervalle entre deux arbaletriers', plate 5 in Matthieu-Prosper Morey (1805–1886), *Charpente de la cathédrale de Messine* (Paris: Didot frères, 1841) Chromolithography printed by Engelmann

Morey toured southern Italy and Sicily in 1836–7 with the architect Victor Baltard (1805–1874). His drawings were engraved and lithographed by Henri Roux, who had published images of ornament from Pompeii and Herculaneum. Morey argued that the roof structure and ornament of Messina Cathedral, which he took to be 12th century, reflected the building and decorative traditions of classical Greece.

19 (RIGHT)

Gherous rug, plate 6 in *Eastern Carpets: Twelve Early Examples*, with descriptive notices by Vincent J. Robinson (London: Henry Sotheran, 1882)

This Kurdish carpet is identified as made by nomad weavers, on account of the boldness of the Persian floral design. Robinson compliments the Kurdish weavers' natural instinct in balancing colour and proportion. The illustrations are printed on grained paper that simulates beautifully the weave of the carpets.

20 (OPPOSITE)

Vatican, third floor interior, plate 3 in Ludwig Grüner (1801–1882), *Fresco Decorations and Stuccoes of Churches & Palaces in Italy, during the Fifteenth & Sixteenth Centuries* (London: J. Murray, 1844)

Grüner's publication was intended to influence those planning the decoration of the new House of Commons after the old building was destroyed by fire in 1834. The work was dedicated to Prince Albert and the members of the Royal Commission on the Fine Arts.

3.

Innere Ansicht von der Gallerie des dritten   §   Vüe interieure de la Gallerie du troisième
Stocks im Hofe der Logen.   Etage, de la cour des Loges.

J. Th.

Frontispiece.

W. Hogarth inv. et delin.   *L. Sullivan Sculp.*

Whoever makes a DESIGN *without the Knowledge of* PERSPECTIVE *will be liable to such Absurdities as are shewn in this* Frontispiece.

21 (OPPOSITE)

John Joshua Kirby (1716–1774),
*Dr Brook Taylor's Method of Perspective
Made Easy: Both in Theory and Practice*
(Ipswich: Printed by W. Craighton
for the author, 1754)

William Hogarth's frontispiece
is deliberately filled with examples
of 'incorrect' linear perspective.
Student designers could avoid
drawing such 'absurdities' by
adhering to Dr Brook Taylor's
method. Brook Taylor's influential
theories on perspective were
disseminated in various works
during the 18th century,
including this illustrated edition
by Joshua Kirby.

22

John Burnet (1784–1868),
*Practical Hints on Colour in Painting:
Illustrated by Examples from the Works
of the Venetian, Flemish and Dutch
Schools*, 5th edn (London: James
Carpenter, 1843)

John Burnet used simplified prints
such as these after paintings by
Rubens, Titian and Van Dyck to
analyse and illustrate the techniques
of the old masters. Several of Burnet's
books for art students focused on
one particular aspect of painting
technique, including this volume
devoted solely to examining the
use of colour.

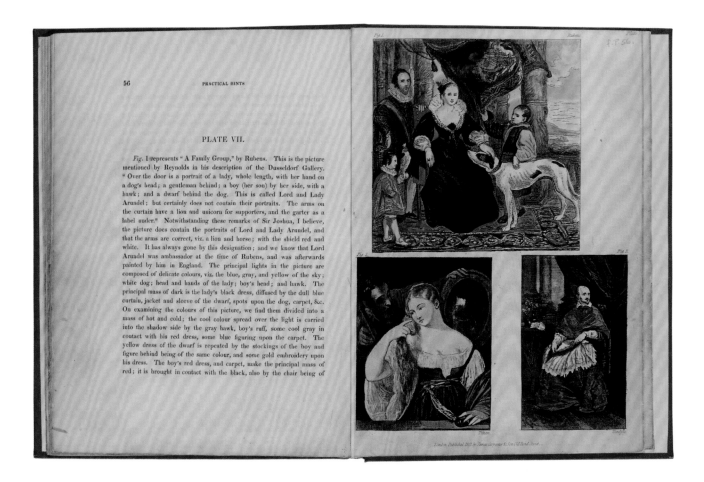

2
Making Images: The Illustrator at Work

Steam presses, the growth of the railways and an increasing population stimulated a publishing boom in the nineteenth century. Lithography, steel engraving and advances in wood engraving meant that by the 1830s society was on the path towards being saturated with images as a means of communication, persuasion and manipulation. Images sold texts, and a wide range of literary, scientific and reference works, as well as periodicals, were published in illustrated editions.

The demand for illustration required image-makers. Some became as famous as the authors they were illustrating: covers would trumpet the name of the artist even above that of the writer. Charles Dickens was famously called in to provide text for images by Robert Seymour (1798–1836) of sporting scenes, treated in a burlesque genre that claimed descent from Rowlandson and Hogarth. The Dickens-Seymour collaboration became *The Pickwick Papers* (published as a monthly series in 1836–7). On Seymour's untimely death, Dickens took full control, recruiting Robert Buss (1804–1875) and then Hablot Knight Browne (1815–1882) to provide images.

In this environment of image-led publication, figures like John Leech, Hablot Knight Browne and George Cruikshank were behind the fortunes of many publishers. Browne adopted the name 'Phiz' when working with Dickens to match the writer's pseudonym 'Boz'. Thackeray provided images and texts for *Punch*, from 1841 among the most successful illustrated periodicals; he acted as both illustrator and writer for many of his own books, so that the images directly supported the messages of the text.

Illustration in the 1860s was dominated by the great firms of the Dalziel Brothers and John Swain & Co. They engraved pictures by some of the most famous artists of the day, and ensured that their work in the form of proofs, printed with greater care than mechanical presses could manage, was lodged in the national collections at the British Museum and the South Kensington Museum.

For coloured illustration, Edmund Evans (1826–1905) was the most successful printer in nineteenth-century Britain before his retirement in 1892. His way of recreating colour drawings, termed 'chromoxylography' (colour printing from woodblocks), brought life and appeal to books, particularly children's books. Alongside his activities as a printer he acted as a publisher, in conjunction with publishers such as Routledge and Warne. Among the artists Evans commissioned were Walter Crane

('He was a genius'), Randolph Caldecott (whom he found a very astute businessman as well as a great artist) and Kate Greenaway (who declared that only Evans could engrave her work). In his autobiography, Evans described his methods of printing, which involved photographing original drawings onto woodblocks and using multiple blocks for different colours to achieve subtleties of coloration on the page. The artwork of these illustrators was collected by the National Art Library from the mid-1880s, and examples appeared in the great *Loan Exhibition of Modern Illustration* held in the Museum in 1901.

Beatrix Potter grew up in South Kensington and developed a close association with the V&A. At the age of 13 she enrolled as a student at the National Art Training School on Exhibition Road. By 1883 she was studying and copying artworks in the Museum's collections and recording her impressions of temporary exhibitions in her journal. Years later, when working on her series of Peter Rabbit books, Potter visited the Library to examine Edmund Evans's wood-engraved proofs to Randolph Caldecott's picture books. Most notably, she copied details of several of the Museum's eighteenth-century costumes in her illustrations to *The Tailor of Gloucester* (1903). Today, the Word and Image Department holds the world's largest collection of Beatrix Potter's correspondence, manuscripts and artwork, much of it collected by Leslie Linder (1904–1973), an engineer and collector, who in 1958 deciphered the code writing in Potter's journal, kept to the age of 30 and revealing observations about life in Victorian Britain.

23 (OPPOSITE, ABOVE)
Thomas Rowlandson (1756–1827)
and William Combe (1742–1823),
The English Dance of Death (London:
R. Ackermann's Repository of Arts,
1815–16)

Combe was commissioned to provide verses (or 'metrical illustrations') to a series of darkly comic pictures by Rowlandson on the subject of death in English society. The illustrations thus preceded the text.

24 (OPPOSITE, BELOW)
Pierce Egan (1772–1849),
Life in London, illustrated by Robert and George Cruikshank (London: Sherwood, Neely and Jones, 1821)

George Cruikshank's first success as a book illustrator was a collaboration with his brother Robert, illustrating Egan's account of the riotous exploits of Jerry Hawthorne and Corinthian Tom (the original Tom and Jerry) in Regency London. The artists and author have been credited with originating the idea, which was at once a best-seller and swiftly pirated.

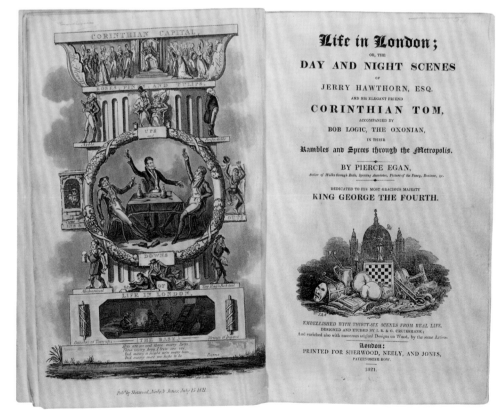

25

Charles Dickens (1812–1870),
Oliver Twist, illustrated by
George Cruikshank (London:
Richard Bentley, 1838)
Bequeathed by John Forster 1876

Oliver Twist was originally serialized
in the monthly magazine *Bentley's
Miscellany*, with one etching by
Cruikshank in each part. This three-
volume edition of the complete
novel was published shortly before
the culmination of the serialization,
thus appearing in a more prestigious
form than a popular magazine.

296   OLIVER TWIST.

of them die,—and joked too, because they died
with prayers upon their lips. With what a
rattling noise the drop went down; and how
suddenly they changed from strong and vigorous
men to dangling heaps of clothes!

Some of them might have inhabited that very
cell—sat upon that very spot. It was very
dark; why didn't they bring a light? The
cell had been built for many years—scores of men
must have passed their last hours there—it was
like sitting in a vault strewn with dead bodies—
the cap, the noose, the pinioned arms—the faces
that he knew even beneath that hideous veil—
Light, light!

At length when his hands were raw with
beating against the heavy door and walls, two
men appeared, one bearing a candle which he
thrust into an iron candlestick fixed against the
wall, and the other dragging in a mattress on
which to pass the night, for the prisoner was to
be left alone no more.

Then came night—dark, dismal, silent night.
Other watchers are glad to hear the church-
clocks strike, for they tell of life and coming

Fagin in the condemned Cell.

26
George Cruikshank (1792–1878),
cover of *Oliver Twist* by Charles Dickens
(London: Bradbury and Evans, 1846)
Bequeathed by Alexander Dyce 1867

Nine years after its first appearance,
Oliver Twist was republished in
monthly parts, the format that had
proved so successful for *The Pickwick
Papers* in 1836–7. For the 1846 issues,
Cruikshank retouched his original
plates and created a cover design
with scenes from the novel, including
a reworked version of Fagin in the
condemned cell.

27
George Cruikshank (1792–1878),
drawing with studies for the
illustration 'Fagin in the Condemned
Cell' and other incidents in the story
of *Oliver Twist* by Charles Dickens,
c.1846
Donated by the artist's widow, Eliza
Cruikshank, 1884

The inscription in Cruikshank's
hand suggests that this was his first
idea for Fagin, but it was probably
written later. The pose of Fagin is
closer to that in the cover design for
the 1846 monthly parts, made eight
years after the original plate.

28
George Cruikshank (1792–1878),
drawing, study for 'Fagin in the
Condemned Cell', *c*.1838
Donated by Eliza Cruikshank

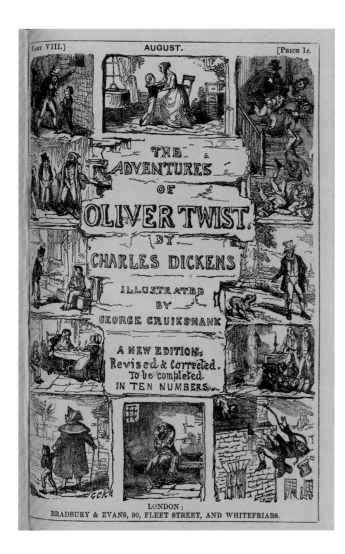

THE BOTTLE.

Plate VII.——THE HUSBAND, IN A STATE OF FURIOUS DRUNKENNESS, KILLS HIS WIFE WITH THE INSTRUMENT OF ALL THEIR MISERY.

THE BOTTLE.

Plate VIII.——THE BOTTLE HAS DONE ITS WORK.—IT HAS DESTROYED THE INFANT AND THE MOTHER. IT HAS BROUGHT THE SON AND THE DAUGHTER TO VICE AND TO THE STREETS, AND HAS LEFT THE FATHER A HOPELESS MANIAC.

29
George Cruikshank (1792–1878),
The Bottle (London: D. Bogue, 1847)
Bequeathed by Chauncy Hare
Townshend 1868

After a hedonistic youth, of the
kind described in *Life in London*
(1821), Cruikshank foreswore drink
and tobacco, championing the cause
of temperance. *The Bottle*, with
its sequel *The Drunkard's Children*,
shows the descent of a family
into murder, prison and suicide,
told in a series of prints in the style
of Hogarth's *Rake's Progress*.

30
George John Pinwell (1842–1875), drawing, original study for 'Leaving the Morgue', illustration to *The Uncommercial Traveller* by Charles Dickens, *c.*1868

31
Dalziel Brothers, after George John Pinwell, proof of 'Leaving the Morgue', illustration for *The Uncommercial Traveller* by Charles Dickens, *c.*1868
Wood engraving

Both preliminary drawing and proof wood engravings were acquired from the Dalziel Brothers, one of the most prolific wood-engraving firms of the period. It was the job of their team of craftsmen to turn the artist's sketch into a woodblock, from which the illustrations could be printed.

32
Charles Dickens (1812–1870), *The Uncommercial Traveller*, illustrated by G.J. Pinwell (London: Chapman and Hall, 1868) Bequeathed by John Forster

Dickens's lively travel pieces had originally appeared without illustrations in *All the Year Round*, the weekly magazine 'conducted by Charles Dickens'. The artist, George Pinwell, was a regular contributor to magazines of the 1860s, and worked with some of the leading firms of wood engravers.

"THIS IS A SWEET SPOT, AIN'T IT? A LOVELLY SPOT!"

33

William Makepeace Thackeray
(1811–1863), *Mrs Perkins's Ball*, 3rd edn
(London: Chapman & Hall, 1847)
Bequeathed by John Forster 1876

Thackeray was an illustrator as well
as an artist. He contributed humorous
illustrated articles to *Punch* and
had applied to Dickens to succeed
Robert Seymour as illustrator of
The Pickwick Papers. His early works
were published under various
pseudonyms, including Michael
Angelo Titmarsh.

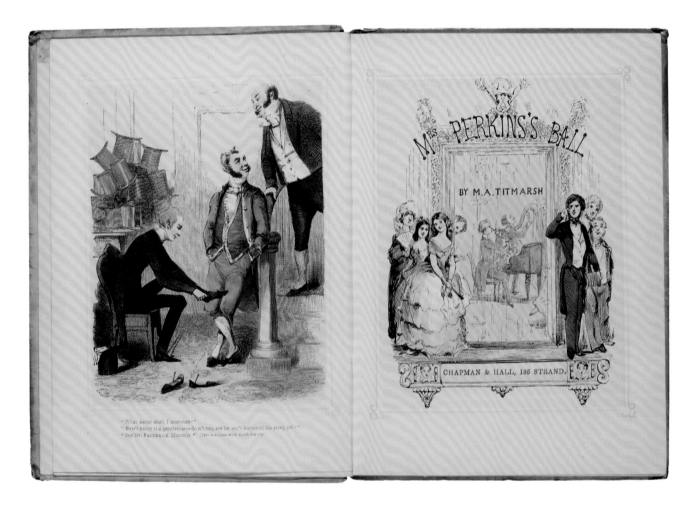

34
Walter Crane (1845–1915),
illustrator, Lucy Crane (1842–1882),
musical arrangements, *Baby's Bouquet:
A Fresh Bunch of Old Rhymes & Tunes*
(London: Warne, 1878)
From the Renier Collection, given
by Anne and Fernand Renier 1970

Crane's distinctive flat, heavily
outlined style was influenced by
traditional Japanese woodcut prints,
by the 1870s available on the London
art market. He was a major figure
of the Arts and Crafts Movement;
this episodic, frieze-like spread is
reminiscent of his work as a designer
of interior furnishings.

35
Walter Crane (1845–1915),
original designs for *The Baby's Bouquet*
Watercolour, *c.*1878
Bought from Lionel Crane 1931

The wood engraver Edmund Evans
engraved and printed Crane's
illustrations, separating the images
into different colours using an ever-
increasing number of woodblocks.
This book of page layouts shows how
Crane produced 'dummies' to plan
each page opening as a complete
unit of design.

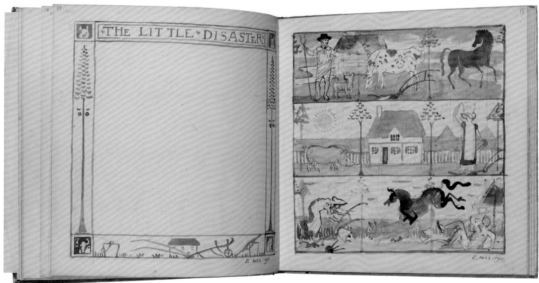

36
Kate Greenaway (1846–1901),
Language of Flowers (London:
Routledge, 1884)
Owned by Beatrix Potter; given by Joan
Duke (donor of a collection of material
owned by Beatrix Potter) 2006

Beatrix Potter's copy of this work
by Kate Greenaway shows an interest
in children's books independent of
the production of her Peter Rabbit
stories. Books about the language
of flowers abounded in Victorian
Britain. The qualities and role
assigned to each flower enabled
a kind of dialogue with nature to
be sustained and messages to be
conveyed between friends.

37
Kate Greenaway (1846–1901),
'Hide and Seek', illustration from
Book of Games (1889)
Watercolour and pen and ink

Greenaway, like Crane, worked
closely with the wood engraver
and printer Edmund Evans. Her
illustrative style portrayed children
in fantastical costumes – mixing
styles from the eighteenth century
and the Arts and Crafts Movement –
inhabiting a clean, sunny and largely
static world.

38
Randolph Caldecott (1846–1886),
watercolour drawing for *A Frog
He Would a Wooing Go, c.*1883
From the bequest of Henry Herbert
Harrod 1948

"Pray, Mr. FROG, will you give us a song?"
Heigho, says ROWLEY!
"But let it be something that's not very long."
With a rowley-powley, gammon and spinach,
Heigho, says ANTHONY-ROWLEY!

39
Randolph Caldecott (1846–1886),
A Frog He Would a Wooing Go
(London: Routledge, 1883)

40

Beatrix Potter (1866–1943),
illustrated manuscript of
The Tale of Mrs Tittlemouse, c.1909
Watercolour and pen and ink
From the bequest of Leslie Linder 1973

Potter was concerned with every
stage of design and production
and had an expert understanding
of the physical make-up of a
book, including the role of the
cover, endpapers, frontispiece and
title page. She produced dummy
manuscripts for her tales to indicate
the precise juxtaposition of text
and image.

41

Beatrix Potter (1866–1943),
preliminary drawing for *The Tale of
Peter Rabbit*, c.1901
Drawing in pencil
From the bequest of Leslie Linder 1973

Potter produced several rough pencil
studies for each illustration before
working up the final versions in
pen and ink. Using real animals as
models, her underlying concern was
always to portray faithfully animal
anatomy and physiognomy.

42 (OPPOSITE)

Beatrix Potter (1866–1943),
illustration for a proposed 'Book
of Rhymes', c.1905
Watercolour and pen and ink
From the bequest of Leslie Linder 1973

Potter recalled eagerly purchasing
Randolph Caldecott's picture books
as a child and claimed her best work
was 'done in imitation'. Her proposed
book of rhymes, in a 'style between
Caldecott's & the Baby's Opera', was
abandoned when her publisher died
in 1905, but she returned to the idea
for *Appley Dapply's Nursery Rhymes*
(1917) and *Cecily Parsley's Nursery
Rhymes* (1922).

3
Designers, Aesthetes and the 'Book Beautiful'

During the last decades of the nineteenth century there was a critical reaction to standards of book design maintained by the publishing industry. In France, designers such as Eugène Grasset (1841–1917), Carlos Schwabe (1866–1926) and Alphonse Mucha (1860–1939) were called in to design books with fashionable modern graphics. A cult of exquisite book production was fostered by critics such as Octave Uzanne (1852–1931) and by private clubs that financed de luxe works made by virtuoso printers and engravers. In Britain, there was a similar reaction to a perceived degeneration and uniformity of the industrially produced book. Charles Ricketts (1866–1931) and Charles Shannon (1863–1937), deeply immersed in French Symbolist art, brought a modern aesthetic to the books of the Vale Press. The sensuous graphics of Aubrey Beardsley (1872–1898), with their exotic association with Japanese prints, Greek vase painting and the Renaissance of Botticelli, soon made him famous after a review in *The Studio* in 1893 and collaboration with the circle of Oscar Wilde (1854–1900); his style was eminently suitable for printing by line blocks.

William Morris (1834–1896) took another route in reconsidering book design. For his Kelmscott Press, he designed his own founts, made his own printers' ink, commissioned new kinds of paper and elaborated his own ornament to match the illustrations of artists such as Walter Crane and Edward Burne-Jones. Kelmscott books prompted many other similar ventures to make up what some call 'the private press movement'. Most presses of this kind followed Morris's example in eschewing what commercial printing and typography had to offer, and were not bound by commercial restraints.

The term the 'book beautiful' was coined by T.J. Cobden-Sanderson (1840–1922), who under the influence of William Morris abandoned a career as a barrister to set up the Doves Press and bindery. C.H. St John Hornby (1867–1946) similarly followed Morris's example with his Ashendene Press, though he did not abandon his career as a director of W.H. Smith. Books produced by such presses aspired to unite the arts of calligraphy, printing, illumination, illustration, binding and decoration to create a single harmonious work – 'the union of all to the production of one composite whole, the consummate Book Beautiful', as Cobden-Sanderson declared.

In 1909 the Library opened its Book Production Gallery to show examples of fine printing, illustration, ornament in books, bookbindings, specimens of famous presses, typical illustrated books and manuscripts with fine writing and illumination. The Library's ambition to display together 'books [acquired] for their own beauty rather than for the information on art matters that they contain' led to a systematic account based on the categories proclaimed in the 1850s. The selection showed the steady nature of the Library's growth, with historic materials acquired alongside books and documents produced as part of Art Nouveau and the Arts and Crafts Movement.

Most of the Library's illuminated manuscripts were displayed (previously, isolated examples had been shown in museum galleries), with a long series of early printed books arranged by country. Near them were Persian and Arabic manuscripts and bindings beloved of both nineteenth-century design reformers and adepts of the Aesthetic Movement. Works of modern European presses collected since the 1880s were also arranged by country. Kelmscott Press books were next to cases with works that showed their impact on British and American production.

In the 1920s the Book Production Gallery was augmented with a display of tools and materials relating to books and bookbinding, a development in which the Central School's Book Production Department played a major part. In 1945 this became the 'Gallery of the Art of the Book'.

43
The Penitential Psalms with an initial showing *David in Penitence*, from a Book of Hours made for Giovanni Bentivoglio, written out by Pierantonio Sallando (active late 15th century). Italy, *c.*1494–1503
Donated by George Reid 1902

Reid had lent 83 illuminated manuscripts for display in the V&A, converting the loan into a gift in 1902 and 1903. He was keen that they be shown to the public: in 1909 he presented six cases for his manuscripts to be included in the Book Production Gallery that opened that year.

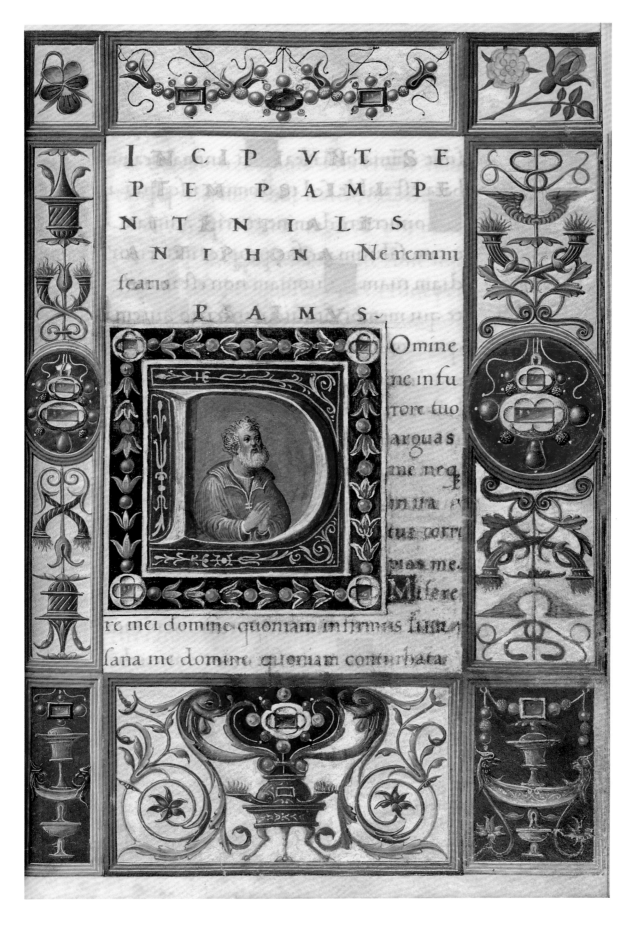

Finito che la nympha cum comitate blandiffima hebbe il fuo beni
gno fuafo & multo acceptiffima recordatióe, che la mia acrocoma Polia
propera & mafuetiffima leuatofe cum gli fui fefteuoli ,& facetiffimi fimu
lachri ,ouero fembianti, & cum punicante gene ,& rubéte buccule da ho
nefto & uenerâte rubore fuffufe aptauafe di uolere per omni uia fatiffare
di natura prompta ad omni uirtute, & dare opera alla honefta petitioné.
Non che prima peroe fe poteffe cælare & dicio retinere alquâto che ella
intrinficamente non fufpirulaffe. Il quale dulciffimo fufpirulo penetroe
reflectendo nel intimo del mio, immo fuo core, per la uniforme conue-
nientia. Quale aduene a dui parimente participati & concordi litui. Et
ciafcuna cum diuo obtuto refpecta intrepidulamente, cum quegli ludi-
bondi & micanti ochii, Da fare (Ome) gli adamanti fref in mille fragmé
ticuli. Cum pie & fummiffe uoce, & cum elegantiffimi gefti decentemen
te reuerita ogni una, ritornoe al fuo folatiofo federe fupra il ferpilaceo fo
lo. La initiata opera fequendo fellularia. Cum accommodata pronunti
atio-

44

Crucifixion scene, from a Book
of Hours made for Margaret de Foix,
wife of the Duke of Brittany
France, c.1471–6
Bequeathed by George Salting 1910

The Salting bequest of 1910
included six outstanding
illuminated manuscripts.
The Margaret de Foix Hours is
usefully dated by the inclusion
of a prayer referring to her sterility.
Her daughter, Anne de Bretagne,
was born on 25 January 1477.

45

Francesco Colonna (1433–1527),
Hypnerotomachia Poliphili
(Venice: Printed by Aldus Manutius,
1499)

This work has long been considered
the apogee of Renaissance
printing, as much on account of
its woodcuts and roman typeface
as the dreamlike, exotic nature of
the love story it contains. Aubrey
Beardsley, Charles Ricketts and
Walter Crane were among its most
articulate admirers.

46 (OPPOSITE)

Binding for a manuscript of the
Khusraw and Shirin of the Persian
poet Nizami Ganjavi (d.1214[?]),
written in nastaliq script
Kashmir, c.1800–29

Indian and Persian ornament had
been included in Owen Jones's
Grammar of Ornament of 1856,
and the Museum had collected
Persian design from its foundation.
This splendidly coloured binding
showed how Persian-style
ornament from Kashmir might
be adapted for a binding to create
a work of exotic luxury.

DESIGNERS, AESTHETES AND THE 'BOOK BEAUTIFUL' 101

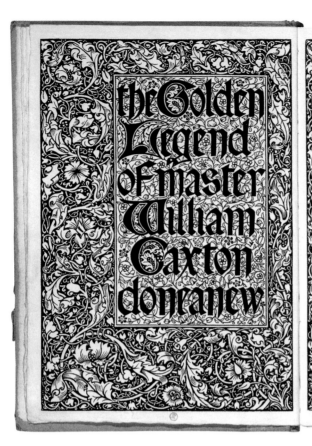

47 (OPPOSITE, ABOVE)
Jacobus de Voragine (*c*.1229–1298), *The Golden Legend of Master William Caxton Done Anew*, designed by William Morris (London: Bernard Quaritch, 1892)

Morris intended this to be the first work printed by the Kelmscott Press, thinking it the crucial text on medieval religious life and thought. Production, however, was delayed due to its length and technical difficulties with the size of the paper; it was handed to the specialist book dealer Bernard Quaritch for publication.

48 (OPPOSITE, BELOW)
William Morris (1834–1896), specimen pages for *The Chronicles of Fraunce, Inglande, and Other Places Adjoynynge*, by Jean Froissart (*c*.1337–*c*.1405) (Hammersmith: Kelmscott Press, 1897)

Lord Berners's 16th-century translation of Froissart's chivalric romances had been a favourite text of Morris's since his college days. A total of 160 copies of these trial pages were issued on vellum to preserve designs made for a projected two-volume folio edition, which was abandoned after Morris's death.

49
Dante Gabriel Rossetti (1828–1882), *The House of Life*, decorated by H.M. O'Kane (New Rochelle, NY: Elston Press, 1901)

The Elston Press was founded in 1900 by Clarke Conwell, a disciple of William Morris. Its publications were all illustrated by Conwell's wife, Helen Marguerite O'Kane (b.1879), in an Art Nouveau style influenced by Burne-Jones. The Press closed in 1905, but was an influential part of the American Arts and Crafts Movement.

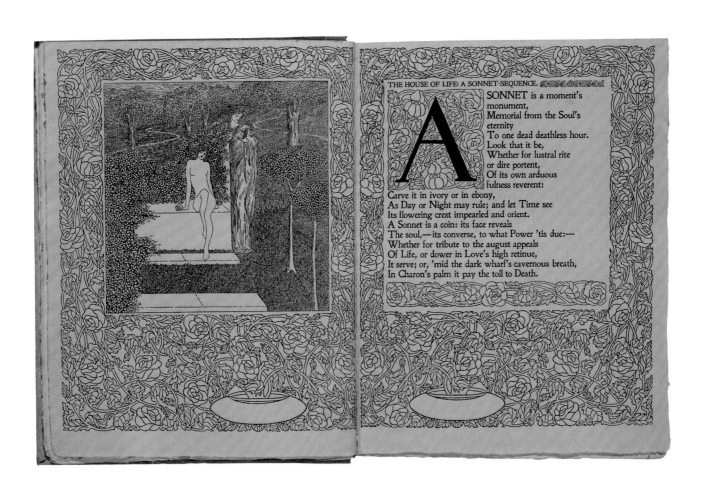

50

The Song of Songs Which is Solomon's, illuminated by Florence Kingsford (1872–1949), with initials by Graily Hewitt (Chelsea: Ashendene Press, 1902)

The overall design of this limited edition of 40 aimed to imitate an illuminated manuscript of the 15th century. Each copy was decorated by hand to an individual design. Several leading women binders bound the copies in differently coloured morocco leather, this copy by Florence Paget.

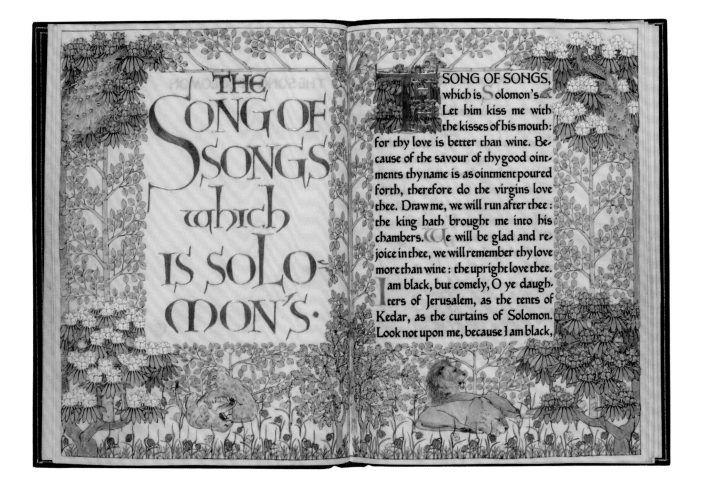

51

Dante Alighieri (1265–1321),
Tutte le opere di Dante Alighieri,
designed by C.H. St John Hornby
(Chelsea: Ashendene Press, 1909)

The Dante published by the
Ashendene Press aspired to rival
the Kelmscott edition of Chaucer
as one of the finest productions by
the British private presses. It was
particularly admired for its page
layout with red initials and devices
designed by the calligrapher Graily
Hewitt (1864–1952).

52

**The Book of Common Prayer, and
Administration of the Sacraments,
& Other Rites & Ceremonies of the
Church, According to the Use of
the Church of England**, designed by
C.R. Ashbee (1863–1942), printed by
the Guild of Handicraft (London: Eyre
& Spottiswoode, 1903)

This was the most ambitious work
produced by the Essex House Press,
formed in 1898 after the Guild of
Handicraft acquired the Kelmscott
Press stock on William Morris's
death. Ashbee had opened the
Guild in 1888 as a cooperative
workshop based in London, before
relocating it to Chipping Campden
in Gloucestershire.

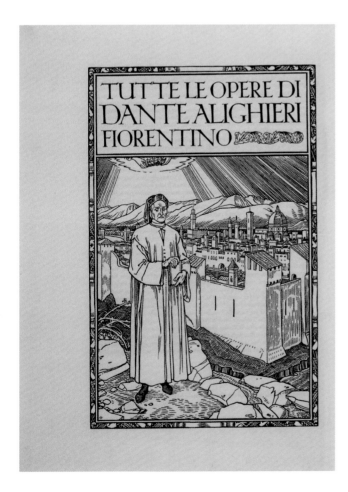

53
Charles Ricketts (1866–1931), cover for Oscar Wilde, *The Sphinx* (London: Elkin Matthews & John Lane, 1894)

Ricketts was responsible for the entire physical appearance of this book, having been commissioned to design the typography, illustrations and binding, as well as select the paper and supervise the printing. He founded his own Vale Press in the mid-1890s to develop his ideas about book design.

54
Aubrey Beardsley (1872–1898), line-block illustration for *Le Morte Darthur* by Thomas Malory (d.1471) (London: J.M. Dent, 1893)

This reprint of Caxton's edition of 1485 was first issued in serial parts. It aimed to show that modern methods could produce fine printing, using the photomechanical line-block process to emulate the expensive woodcut technique of the Kelmscott Press.

55
Aubrey Beardsley (1872–1898), line-block prints for chapter headings of *Le Morte Darthur* by Thomas Malory (London: J.M. Dent, 1893)

This was Beardsley's first professional commission, which required more than 1,000 decorative designs. He tired of the project and produced mock-medieval illustrations that imitated the Kelmscott style to the point of parody, much to Morris's displeasure.

56
Aubrey Beardsley (1872–1898),
line-block print for Oscar Wilde,
Salomé (London: Elkin Mathews
& John Lane, 1894)

Beardsley's drawings for Wilde's
play introduced a Symbolist flavour
to British illustration, at odds with
the Arts and Crafts ethos. Beardsley
preferred photomechanical processes
to traditional wood engraving in order
to enhance the effect of his bold use
of black and white.

57

Will Bradley (1868–1962),
cover design for Stephen Crane
(1871–1900), *War is Kind*
(New York: F.A. Stokes, 1899)

As a pioneer of American poster art,
Bradley popularized a style of Art
Nouveau illustration that was often
compared with Beardsley's work.
The influence of Charles Ricketts,
however, is more apparent in the
harsh, linear designs of this book
(which Bradley considered to be his
masterpiece).

58

Histoire des Quatre Fils Aymon,
designed by Eugène Grasset
(1841–1917), using
chromotypogravure for the
illustration (Paris: H. Launette, 1883)

This book was commissioned to
demonstrate the new technique
of photolithography, pioneered
by Charles Gillot, which allowed
the layout of type and illustration
to be photographed and printed
in colour simultaneously. This
innovative form of production
almost bankrupted the publisher,
but by 1900 it was an icon of
fashionable book design.

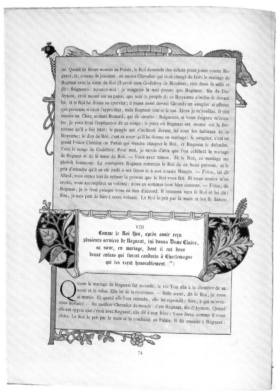

59

Eugène Grasset (1841–1917),
colour lithographed poster for
Encre L. Marquet (Paris: G. de
Malherbe, 1892)

Exhibitions of French posters were
held in London in 1894 and 1895,
not in an art gallery but in a music
hall called 'the Royal Aquarium'.
The Library bought several posters
by artists whose work in books and
prints was already in its collections.

60

Ilsée, princesse de Tripoli,
by Robert de Flers, with colour
lithographed illustration by
Alphonse Mucha (1860–1939)
(Paris: H. Piazza, 1897)

Mucha was commissioned to
illustrate this adaptation of
Edmond Rostand's play *La princesse
Lointaine* (1895), for which he had
designed the set and costumes.
Mucha converted his studio into
a lithographic workshop, working
directly onto stone blocks. He then
hand-painted the proofs to intensify
the colours of his exotic designs.

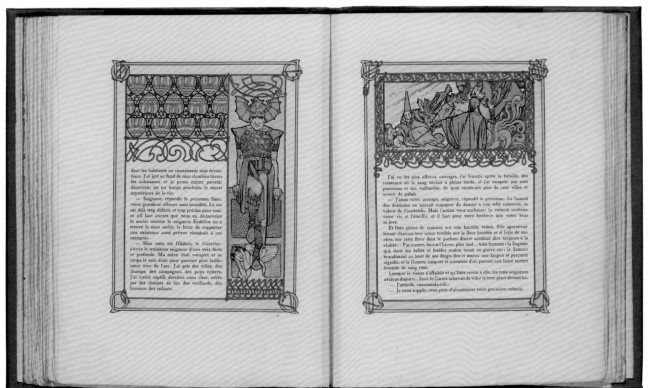

61

Pierre Bonnard (1867–1947),
colour lithographed poster for
L'estampe et l'affiche (Paris: Edouard
Pelletan, 1897)

Bonnard's first appearance in
the V&A's collections was as
an illustrator and poster artist –
works by Bonnard otherwise entered
British public collections only
in the 1920s. This poster may have
been acquired to draw attention
to the Library's collection of prints
and posters.

62

Louis Rhead (1857–1926),
cover for Octave Uzanne,
*L'art dans la decoration exterieure
des livres, en France et a l'étranger*
(Paris: Société Française d'Editions
d'Art, 1897)

Rhead studied at the National Art
Training School in South Kensington
before establishing himself in the
United States as a graphic artist.
Enthused by the work of Grasset,
he turned to posters in the 1890s
and held one-man shows of his
designs in New York, London and
Paris. Uzanne was an arbiter of
taste in the bibliophile circles that
flourished in France – and which
published quantities of de luxe
illustrated books – from the 1880s.

63
Georges Canape (1864–1940),
goatskin binding for Joseph Bédier,
Le roman de Tristan et Iseut
(Paris: H. Piazza, 1900)

The floral aesthetic (*le flore stylisé*)
of this binding shows the influence
of the innovative Marius-Michel
bindery, which advocated a harmony
between the exterior and interior of
the book. This Art Nouveau style in
binding design was celebrated at the
Paris Exposition Universelle of 1900.

64
Sarah Treverbian Prideaux
(1853–1933), goatskin binding of 1902
for Edward Fitzgerald, *Rubaiyat of Omar
Khayyam of Naishapur*, designed
by Charles Ricketts (London: Hacon
and Ricketts, 1901)

This is one of the last bindings
designed by Prideaux, executed by
the trade binder Lucien Broca. It was
inspired by Turkish and Syrian tiles
held in the V&A. Prideaux's binding
tools were donated to the Museum
and put on display in the Book
Production Gallery in 1921.

4
The Impact of Photography: Extending the Encyclopedia

The new museum set up after the Great Exhibition of 1851 sought to give an encyclopedic account of the world of art and design. Where the acquisition of original works was not possible, facsimiles in many forms were acquired, photographs chief among them.

Photography was first introduced to a wide audience with the publications of Louis Daguerre (1787–1851) in 1838 and William Fox Talbot (1800–1877) in 1844. Industry soon found practical applications for this revolutionary technology. Photographs recorded the Great Exhibition of 1851, with its triumphal display of advances in manufacturing, and these were used to illustrate an edition of the exhibition's Reports by the Juries. Photographic techniques soon became a widely used method for illustration, the qualities of verisimilitude prized, for example, for pictures of objects and buildings, as well as landscapes.

The South Kensington Museum provided photographs of what it collected as early as 1859. Charles Thurston Thompson (1818–1868) became the photographer for the new museum as the 'Superintendent of Photography'. Photographs were also commissioned of buildings, monuments and artworks in continental Europe and beyond.

Photography aided scientific research, as with the celebrated work by Eadweard Muybridge, *Animal Locomotion* (1887), in which 781 folio-sized plates analysed precisely how humans and animals moved their limbs. But photography was also claimed as an art in its own right, one that could rival painting and drawing. Francis Frith in 1859 declared that distinguished photography required 'much greater acquaintance with the principles of Art than would seem to be applicable to a merely mechanical science'. The photographs of Julia Margaret Cameron (1815–1879), acquired in 1865, certainly fell into the category of Art. There was disagreement among photographers about how photographs were to be evaluated. Peter Henry Emerson, for instance, entered into acrimonious public debate with George Davison, Henry Peach Robinson and others about the nature of this new art.

65
Charles Thurston Thompson
(1818–1868), albumen print of a Venetian mirror of *c.*1700 from the collection of John Webb, 1853

Thurston Thompson photographed many art objects, 'primarily to furnish models for the use of the eighty art schools in connexion with the Department of Science and Art'. The photograph displays an ornate Venetian mirror, in which the photographer himself is reflected.

66

Charles Thurston Thompson
(1818–1868), albumen print
of a maiolica plate (now V&A:
7165–1860) 'with a portrait
of Perugino', one of many
photographs of the Soulages
Collection, 1856

Charles Thurston Thompson was
sent to Toulouse to photograph
the collection of the French lawyer
Jules Soulages. Following Soulages's
death in 1857, the Museum acquired
the collection in instalments
between 1859 and 1865 for £11,000.
The association with the painter
Perugino was soon shown to be
groundless.

67

Charles Thurston Thompson
(1818–1868), photograph of a
maiolica plate showing an allegory
of love (now V&A: 1806–1855),
in *Photographic Illustrations of Works
in Various Sections of the Collection*
(London: South Kensington Museum,
1859)

Charles Thurston Thompson, the
first official photographer in any
museum, photographed museum
objects chosen by J.C. Robinson.
The maiolica plate shown was
selected from an already large
ceramics collection; it was made
in Deruta, Italy, between 1480 and
1500, and acquired by the Museum
in 1855.

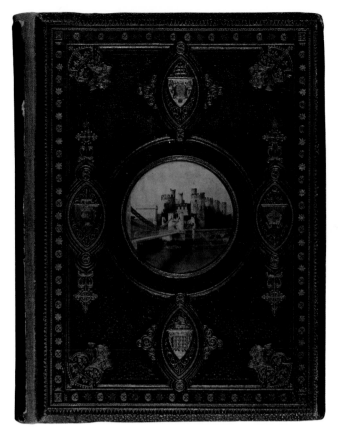

DUNGEON-GHYLL, LANGDALE.
P. 37.

68
William Russell Sedgfield
(1826–1902), albumen photograph
of Conway Castle in William and
Mary Howitt, *Ruined Abbeys and
Castles of Great Britain*, with 26
mounted photographs by Francis
Bedford, George Washington Wilson,
Roger Fenton, Thomas Ogle and others
Second series (London: A.W. Bennett,
1862)

The title of the book reflects at
once an enthusiasm for medieval
architecture seen as romantic
ruins, and a concern for realism
and literal accuracy. Conway Castle
was atypical in not being a ruin.
The illustrations were the work
of the foremost photographers of
the day, their work rivalling prints
and paintings.

69
Thomas Ogle (1813–1882),
photograph of Dungeon Ghyll,
Langdale, for *Our English Lakes,
Mountains and Waterfalls, as seen
by William Wordsworth*, with
photographs by Thomas Ogle
(London: A.W. Bennett, 1864)

Originally trained as a bookbinder,
and a teacher of landscape and
figurative drawing at evening classes,
Thomas Ogle became a professional
portrait photographer. He later
specialized in the photography of
scenic views, particularly in the
Lake District. As was usual in mid-
19th-century books, the photographs
were pasted in by hand.

2. THE WEST FRONT OF THE CHURCH AND THE CAPELLA DO FUNDADOR.

70
Charles Thurston Thompson
(1818–1868), photograph of the west
front of the church and the Capella
do Fundador in *The Sculptured
Ornament of the Monastery of Batalha
in Portugal* (London: Arundel Society
for Promoting the Knowledge of
Art, 1868)

Volumes from this series were
intended for the education
of art students. The series was
a collaboration between the
Museum, the Science and Art
Department and the Arundel
Society. Photographers were sent
to noteworthy buildings throughout
Europe. The Arundel Society dealt
with the business aspect, while
the Museum made space available
for publications to be advertised.

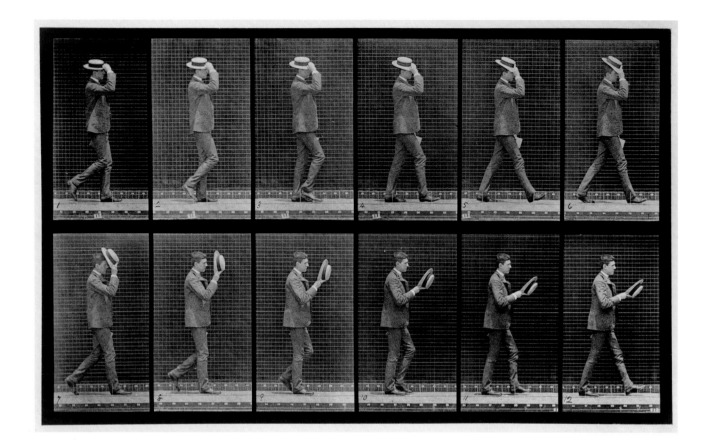

71

Eadweard Muybridge (1830–1904),
collotype photograph of a man taking
off his boater, in *Animal Locomotion*
(Philadelphia: University
of Pennsylvania, 1887)

Aiming to analyse animal
movement, Muybridge was the
first person to make convincing
photographs of small fractions of
time, anticipating the invention
of film. He became famous for
proving that horses galloped with
four feet simultaneously off the
ground. The South Kensington
Museum subscribed to the complete
set of *Animal Locomotion* plates – 781
in all – analysing animal and human
movement.

The Impact of Photography: Reportage

Publishers soon began to publicize the fact that images in books and magazines were based on photographs rather than artists' sketches, lauding the ability of photographs to give a vivid and supposedly realistic account of objects, people, places and dramatic situations. Roger Fenton (1819–1869) contrasted the reality and veristic detail of his own landscape photography taken during the Crimean War in 1855 with the sketchy impressions of the artist Edward A. Goodall (1819–1908). Images produced by both men were published as wood engravings in the *Illustrated London News* and helped fuel public anger at the conduct of the war. Photography became the usual method for swift transfer of images onto woodblocks, so that after the engraver had done his or her work they could be printed with text.

The development of half-tone and photogravure technologies from the late 1880s allowed direct reproduction of photographs, so that the images in magazines such as *The Sketch*, first published in 1893, were made entirely of photomechanically produced line blocks and half-tone plates. The invention of portable hand-held cameras with fast shutter speeds soon enabled action to be recorded spontaneously. From the late nineteenth century, cheap magazines filled with photographic images had very wide circulation.

In the twentieth century densely illustrated magazines could become instruments of persuasion relaying political messages.

The propaganda potential of such publications can be seen clearly in Germany during the Weimar and Nazi years, where illustrated magazines supported political groups promoting rival ideologies. A major collection of such publications was acquired by the National Art Library in 1993 from Colin Osman, editor of *Creative Camera* magazine, and Tim Gidal, a founding figure in modern photojournalism.

Photographers working as journalists became celebrities. Their names and individual styles helped to sell the periodicals in which their work appeared. Social events and accounts of contemporary everyday life provided as much work as wars, accidents and state occasions. Photographers such as Bill Brandt, Lee Miller and André Kertész worked on a freelance basis. In 1947 the photographers Robert Capa, Henri Cartier-Bresson, George Rodger and David 'Chim' Seymour set up the photographic agency Magnum so that they could work in a cooperative manner and rely on the agency's staff to service their activities. Photographs from any single campaign might be published together in a book, or sold and published either individually or as a selection in, for example, a magazine.

Photo-based magazines from Soviet Russia during the Cold War, and from China during the Cultural Revolution, give a vivid account through photographic images of the official view of social progress.

72
Bill Brandt (1904–1983),
'Parlour maid and under parlour maid ready to serve dinner'
Gelatin silver print, 1933; printed 1977

The son of a German mother and a British father, Brandt came to Britain in 1933. This photograph comes from a campaign exploring aspects of British society and customs.

73 (OPPOSITE, ABOVE)
Bill Brandt (1904–1983), *The English at Home* (London: Batsford, 1936)

Once in England, Brandt initially produced two photo books: *The English at Home* (1936) and *A Night in London* (1938). Page openings often capture the contrasting lifestyles of different parts of British society.

74 (OPPOSITE, BELOW)
Bill Brandt (1904–1983), photographs in *Picture Post*, 29 July 1939 (London: Hulton Press, 1939)

Following his flight from Nazi Germany, the Jewish photojournalist and film-maker Stefan Lorent founded the innovative and highly successful photo-based British magazine *Picture Post*. Shots from Brandt's photo shoot of 1933 are developed here into a feature, 'A Parlour Maid's Day'.

Regency Homes in Mayfair 5 Maisons de Mayfair

"Dinner is Served" 6 "Madame est servie"

1.30 p.m. *She Waits at Luncheon*
Waiting at table is the most important of a parlourmaid's duties. When the family lunches on the loggia, Pratt has the assistance of an under-parlourmaid; but it will take her years to master Pratt's perfect technique.

Choosing the Silver
From the wide selection of silver in the pantry safe, Pratt chooses the appropriate pieces for the dinner-table. One of her duties is to take the key of the safe up to bed with her every night.

Night-caps for the Drawing-room
Like a butler, Pratt has the key of the wine cellar. She is responsible for the decanting, and the correct serving, of wines. Punctually at ten each night she brings up the whisky and sodas and the beer.

5.0 p.m. *She Does a Little Sewing*
In her spare time, and in her own room, she may make anything that she pleases. When she left school she had the opportunity of learning millinery, but instead she went into domestic service, as a pantrymaid.

3.30 p.m. *She Lays the Dinner Table*
No sooner is luncheon cleared than the parlourmaid, assisted by her under-parlourmaid, lays the table for dinner. Centre of the table is left to Pratt who has a different arrangement for each day of the month.

Taking Her Afternoon Off
Every Wednesday Pratt has her "half day." She leaves at noon and makes straight for London, whence she visits friends at Putney. She does a little shopping, sees a film, and is back again by 10.30.

Sees that the House is Safe
Pratt is the main custodian of the safety, as well as of the interests, of the "family." While the visitors play a game of poker in the lounge Pratt makes a round of the house, setting the burglar alarms and bolting the outside doors.

6.0 p.m. *Setting the Details of the Menu for Dinner*
Closeted in the kitchen with the cook, Pratt holds a last-minute consultation about the items in the dinner menu. Pratt and the cook, who is also an upper servant, address each other on terms of equality.

4.0 p.m. *She Writes a Letter Home*
Most of the spare time in the afternoon Pratt spends in her sitting-room, mending socks and shirts for the gentlemen of the household. Still, every now and then, there is time for a letter home.

give instructions. She learned all those mysterious unwritten laws governing the duties of the various members of the staff. That as a parlourmaid, she must dust only the tops of the writing-tables. A housemaid does the lower parts. And that a parlourmaid does not sweep up the cake crumbs left on the drawing-room carpet, unless she can do so immediately after tea. If left until later, they must be tidied by a housemaid.

Proud of her profession and jealous of its traditions, Pratt directs the other maids like a general in charge of an army. Nothing escapes her duck and inscrutable eyes. Everything about her is impeccably correct. Grown-ups are frightened to misbehave in front of her. Small boys

adore her because she calls them "Sir." She possesses that Victorian spirit of loyalty to the "family," and has made their interests hers.

Pratt thinks big dinner parties very interesting, and enjoys the "family's" entertaining, in spite of the extra work. She knows everybody's likes and dislikes. Even after his or her first visit to the house, a guest's individual preferences are remembered.

A head-parlourmaid finds her own under-parlourmaids and pantrymaids. Pratt says that this is becoming increasingly difficult. She speaks disapprovingly of modern girls. They are not sufficiently interested to take the long training necessary for her own specialised work and prefer to become ordinary "general" maids instead.

8.0 p.m. *The End of a Parlourmaid's Day*
She is present in the dining-room throughout the meal. She hears every word that is spoken, yet she does not hear it. She is the essence of discretion and tact, the stately parlourmaid of England.

46 47

75
'Das Neuste fürs Baby',
in *Arbeiter Illustrierte Zeitung*, 11 July 1935
(Prague: P Prokop, 1935)

The *Arbeiter Illustrierte Zeitung* was one
of the first anti-Fascist publications,
published in Berlin from 1927 until
1933, and in Prague after its expulsion
from Germany until 1936. The
powerful emotive covers suggest the
consequences of Germany's war-
mongering activities, with an image of
children being kitted out in gas masks.

76
**'Getragen von der Liebe des ganzen
Volkes'**, in *Illustrierter Beobachter*,
27 April 1939 (Munich: F. Eher Nachf, 1939)
From the Osman Gidal Collection

The Nazi Party exploited the power of
photographic images for propaganda
purposes. Their photo-based weekly
magazine featured many images of Hitler.
This issue is a special edition providing
a commemorative career in pictures for
Hitler's fiftieth birthday by the Nazi's
official photographer, Heinrich Hoffmann.

77
Georg Buderose (ed.),
England so- und so! (Berlin: Scherl, 1939)

This Nazi photo book was designed
to show German citizens the 'real'
England. Views of the British
treatment of its colonial territories
and the unemployed are contrasted
with privileged scenes of the upper
echelons of society, predominantly
focusing on Jewish figures.

Berliner
Illustrirte Zeitung

Londoner Morgen
Herbst 1940

79
USSR in Construction
(English edition of *SSSR na stroĭke*),
no. 2, 1933 [16th year of Russian
Revolution] (Moscow: State Publishing
House of Graphic Arts, 1933)

The official view of Soviet society
was effectively captured in these
dramatic photographic images. *SSSR
na stroĭke* was published in English,
French and German editions between
1930 and 1949. It was succeeded
by *VD Voskresenie* (English edition:
Soviet Union), which ran until 1992,
published also in Chinese and Spanish.

78
'Londoner Morgen, Herbst 1940',
in *Berliner Illustrirte Zeitung*, 10 October
1940 (Berlin: Ullstein & Co., 1940)
From the Osman Gidal Collection

Magazines making full use of
photogravure and relief half-tone
processes emerged shortly after 1900.
Images were vastly more prominent
than text. The compact German
Ermanox, Leica and, later, the
Contax cameras, eminently portable
and capable of taking pictures
spontaneously, revolutionized
photography during the Weimar
years in Germany (1919–33) and
elsewhere. The results of this
practicality can be seen here in
clandestine shots taken on enemy
soil during the London Blitz of 1940.

80
China Pictorial
(English edition of *Ren min hua bao*),
7/8 (Beijing: China Pictorial, July–
August 1971)

China Pictorial is an English-language
edition of a predominantly image-
based Chinese periodical. During
the period of the Cultural Revolution,
efficient and contented soldiers and
workers would often be shown in
groups or as single iconic images to
a native as well as a foreign audience.

The Impact of Photography: Photography as Art

The use of photography as an expressive artistic medium can be traced back to its earliest years. In 1858 the South Kensington Museum held the first exhibition of the art of photography to be held in any museum. The Library began a process of systematically collecting work by the most distinguished photographers of the day, among them Francis Bedford (1816–1894), Roger Fenton (1819–1869), Edouard-Denis Baldus (1813–1889) and Charles Nègre (1820–1880). Along with carefully constructed portraiture came works depicting landscapes in a way that rivalled painting, striking accounts of architecture and scenes of human activities loaded with powerful messages. Some of this work appeared in books. In the twentieth century celebrated photographers published their work in books that they themselves designed, the form of the book giving control over the way the images were approached and the links between them. In 1977 single-print photographs of an artistic nature were selected from the National Art Library's holdings to form today's Photographic Section of the Word and Image Department. Its collections are developed alongside the Library's collection of photo books.

81
Peter Henry Emerson (1856–1936), *Pictures of East Anglian Life* (London: Sampson Low, Marston, Searle & Rivington, 1888)

Emerson held that proper manipulation of photographic images could produce an independent art whose rules had nothing to do with painting or drawing. His balanced compositions are constructed with areas of both sharp and soft focus, to match the workings of the human eye. He produced his own photogravures, dissatisfied with what was available commercially. His bucolic subject matter records a fading agrarian way of life.

82
Julia Margaret Cameron
(1815–1879), photograph of the poet
Tennyson, in Anne Thackeray Ritchie,
*Alfred Lord Tennyson and his Friends:
A Series of 25 Portraits in Photogravures
from the Negatives of Mrs Julia Margaret
Cameron and H.H.H. Cameron*
(London: T. Fisher Unwin, 1893)

Cameron photographed Tennyson
on several occasions. She donated
a portrait to the South Kensington
Museum in 1865. In that same year,
the Museum was the first institution
to exhibit her work. Her portraits
prized artistry over realism.

83
Man Ray (1890–1976),
*La photographie n'est pas l'art:
12 photographies* (Paris: Editions
GLM, 1937)

Man Ray felt that the critical
acclaim for his photography
detracted attention from his
painting. In this book he reacted
to this success by placing
commercially commissioned
photographs in a photo-book
format and imbuing them
with new meaning through
provocative captions.

*D*ans les yeux des autres

*L*e sex-appeal

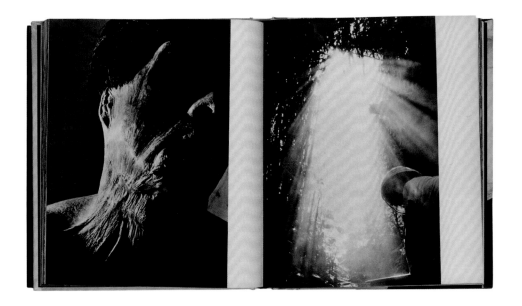

84

Shōmei Tōmatsu (1930–2012),
‹11.02› *Nagasaki* (Tokyo: Shashin
Dōjinsha, 1966)

In 1960 Tōmatsu was asked by the
Japan Council against Atomic Bombs
to document the effects of the atomic
explosion that had devastated
Nagasaki in 1945. His photographs
of scarred humans and damaged
objects appear even more poignant
when viewed alongside his images of
a city in the midst of reconstruction.

85

Eikō Hosoe (b.1933),
Kamaitachi (Tokyo: Gendai
Shichōsha, 1969)

Hosoe photographed the dancer
Tatsumi Hijikata's recreation of
the Japanese folk legend 'Kamaitachi'
(a 'yōkai', or supernatural monster,
associated with devilish winds).
Hijikata conveys Kamaitachi as a
whirling dervish causing mayhem
throughout the countryside. Each
black-and-white image is housed in
a vivid blue gatefold, accentuating a
ritualistic aspect common to much
of Hosoe's work. This ensures that
the book is revealed slowly, forcing
the reader to linger over the images.

86

Eikō Hosoe (b.1933),
*Barakei: shinshūban / Ordeal by Roses:
Re-edited* (Tokyo: Shūeisha, 1971)

The collaboration between Hosoe
and the writer Yukio Mishima
resulted in dark photogravures
depicting Mishima in various poses
exploring violence, sex and death.
This 're-edited' version (*Barakei* was
originally published in 1963) was
designed by Tadanori Yakoo, who
was responsible for the additional
colour illustrations, including the
book's flamboyant fold-out cover.

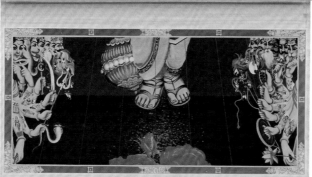

The playing fields of Tladi, Soweto. August 1972.

Miss Lovely Legs Competition at the Pick 'n Pay Hypermarket, Boksburg 1980.

87
David Goldblatt (b.1930),
South Africa (London: Photographers'
Gallery, 1986)
Photograph by David Goldblatt

Goldblatt made a series of
explorations of his native South
African society, both during and
after apartheid. From a balanced
viewpoint, critical but not
judgemental, he here juxtaposed
images of everyday life in black
and white communities.

88
Stephen Gill (b.1971),
Hackney Wick (London: Nobody Books,
in association with Archive of Modern
Conflict, 2005)

From a market in Hackney Wick,
east London, Gill bought for 50p
a plastic camera with no focus or
exposure control, and used it to
record the changes in the area,
transformed by redevelopment for
the 2012 Olympic Games.

89
Martin Parr (b.1952),
Benidorm Album (Bristol[?]:
Martin Parr, 1997)

Parr is known for his intimate
depictions of the British,
transforming everyday life into
vividly coloured conversation
pieces. An artist's proof (one of
only eight copies), this collection
of holiday resort photographs has
been mocked up in the style of
an 'ordinary' holiday album.

90
Christien Meindertsma (b.1980),
Checked Baggage: 3264 Prohibited Items
(Eindhoven: Soeps Uitgeverij, 2004)

Inspired by the impact of
11 September 2001 on airport
security, Meindertsma categorized
a week's worth of objects confiscated
from Schiphol Airport outside
Amsterdam. She photographed all
3,264 items (ranging from souvenir
corkscrews to toy guns) on a pristine
white background. Each photo book
is accompanied by one of these
'dangerous' objects.

5
Promoting Commercial Art: The Initiative of 1936

As the world recovered painfully from the financial crash of 1929–30, heightened attention was paid to the way in which commercial art could encourage economic activity. International trade exhibitions were held in an effort to stimulate commercial growth, and advertising campaigns were organized with innovative graphics to encourage consumption. Cyril Connolly (1903–1974) saw hope in such activities. In his review of the Shell-Mex advertising exhibition at the New Burlington Gallery in London in 1934, he referred to the 'new Medici', a network of influential people associated with commercial art that included Paul Nash, Kenneth Clark, Walter Gropius, Clive Bell, Jack Beddington, Ashley Havinden, Frank Pick and Beatrice Warde, the last being the publicity manager of the Monotype Corporation Ltd. The Royal Academy exhibition *Art and Industry* (1936) was less sanguine. In stressing the link between effective design and commercial success, it stated that for British goods 'the flower of our national pride has lately shown signs of wilting, if only for the lack of the fertilising effect of the imagination'.

In 1936, in the influential journal *Penrose Annual*, Beatrice Warde (1900–1969) described an imaginary box of 'jobs' that would display noteworthy new developments in printing. As if in response, in May that year Philip James (1901–1974), Deputy Keeper of the National Art Library, began a process of requesting samples of work from significant designers across Europe and North America. He aimed to complement the Library's extensive holdings of journals and books on the theory and practice of commercial art, such as Leon Friend's *Graphic Design*, which demonstrated techniques with images of contemporary printing. James's development of the collection took this approach further, providing students with handling examples of different methods, styles and stages in the printing process. The intention was to create an 'open reference collection of commercial typography [so that] the trend of typographic design, both in [Britain] and abroad, could be appraised by students of industrial art'. What was gathered

would 'catch the eye and stimulate the senses', while also exposing students to work from the Continent that 'responds far more quickly to current movements in art and design than does the work produced in [Britain]'. Philip James's view that commercial art was an essential factor not only in business ('success is dependent on the graphic artists and not the office boy') but also in shaping consumer taste recalls some of the founding principles of the Museum.

A small exhibition, *Modern Commercial Typography*, was held in the V&A's Book Gallery to publicize the new collection in 1936. Distinctive examples of current but traditional work were displayed next to material that showed the influence of Constructivism, Surrealism, Vorticism and other avant-garde movements. Work produced for commercial organizations was shown next to that commissioned, for instance, by the Public Relations Department of Britain's General Post Office. The latter was innovative in commissioning artists for its printed publicity rather than using advertising agencies. Much of what was sent to the National Art Library reflected progressive developments in architecture and photography, where dynamic simplicity was valued over detail, form preferred to ornament, and where typography was used as an illustrative element. On the production side, much material shows the use of new techniques such as airbrushing and photomontage.

The collection made by Philip James brought in work that captured a complex and exciting moment in the evolution of commercial art in Britain. Many commercial artists sent in a selection of what they had done earlier in their career, but the bulk dates from the time of James's requests, that is to say 1936 and 1937. Today the collection, consisting of perhaps some 6,000 items, is known as the 'Jobbing Printing Collection'. A sympathetic response from the printing industry can be seen in the reaction of the great typographer Stanley Morison (1889–1967), who from this date began sending in typographic specimens, scrapbooks and publications as gifts to the Library.

The text visible within the image:

10

The
INFLUENCE
of
MODERN LIFE
on
Present day
LAY-OUT

If certain people have defined the modern style as an absence of style, it is only because style to-day has adopted a different habit from that by which it used to be recognised.

The demise of ornament has not brought style into the grave. It is characteristic of the art of our time that it oversteps conventional limits. It stands on the threshold of new discoveries. It is intimately connected with science, and what one arbitrarily terms Art is a very arbitrary thing indeed, if it excludes the graphic, photographic, phonographic, radiophonic, and cinematographic arts.

Another factor besides our scientific turn of mind has helped to determine the modern style. This factor may be termed overcrowding. The lack of time and lack of space, which the incessant increase of our wants brings home to us more and more every day, have forced the arts to adopt a new mode of life, or rather to adapt themselves to the change in our own mode of life.

91
Alfred Tolmer (1876–1957),
Mise en page: Theory and Practice of Lay-out (London: The Studio Ltd, 1931)

Tolmer's experimental and sought-after primer about layout (the arrangement of text and images on a page) demonstrated new graphic possibilities. Works of this kind in the Library anticipated the initiative of 1936 to bring together a Jobbing Printing Collection.

92

Exhibition 1933: The Advertising and Marketing Exhibition, Olympia, London, July 17–22, designed by Ashley Havinden (1903–1973) (London: Advertising Association, 1933)

The Olympia exhibition of 1933 was a response to agreements signed in Ottawa in 1932 to revive commercial activity within the Commonwealth in 'defiance of world depression'. The Advertising Association's pamphlet encouraged global participation. Havinden was a major influence in British advertising, responsible for memorable advertising campaigns for the Milk Marketing Board, Simpson's of Piccadilly and others.

93

Herbert Bayer (1900–1985), typed manuscript letter from Bayer to Philip James concerning the donation of material to the Jobbing Printing Collection Germany, 1937

Both the letterhead and the text in this response from Herbert Bayer demonstrate his maxim that the use of upper-case letters is unnecessary – a powerful statement as regards the German language.

94 (OPPOSITE, ABOVE)

Herbert Bayer (1900–1985), proof sheet for *Universal Alphabet* Dessau, c.1926

In 1925 the founder of the Bauhaus, Walter Gropius, asked Bayer, Head of the Printing and Advertising Department, to design a new typeface for all the school's printing. Bayer reduced the alphabet to its essential lines and curves, resulting in a more legible text and a cleaner look.

95 (OPPOSITE, BELOW)

Bauhaus student work, example of hand-lettered typeface Dessau, c.1925–30

Fundamental to Bauhaus principles was that all students should master lettering in their first year. This example by a student of Jan Tschichold quotes Schiller's 'Song of the Bell'.

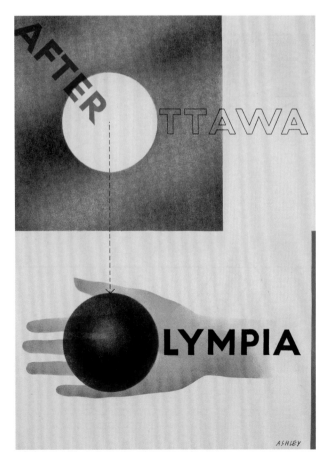

abcdefghi
jklmnopqr
stuvwxyz

HERBERT BAYER: Abb. 1. Alfabet
„g" und „k" sind noch als
unfertig zu betrachten

Beispiel eines Zeichens
in größerem Maßstab
Präzise optische Wirkung

sturm blond

Abb. 2. Anwendung

WOHLTÄTIG IST DES FEUERS MACH
T, WENN SIE DER MENSCH BEZÄMT, B
EWACHT UND WAS ER BILDET, WAS
ER SCHAFFT, DAS DANKT ER DIESER
HIMMELSKRAFT. DOCH FURCHTBAR
WIRD DIE HIMMELSKRAFT WENN SIE
DER FESSEL SICH ENTRAFFT, EINERTR
ITT AUF DER EIGNEN SPUR, DIE FREIE

3

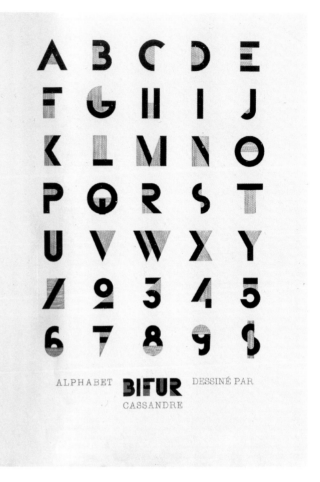

96
Jan Tschichold (1902–1974),
proof for the poster *Statistik der ehe
Scheidungen in Deutschland im ehe Buch*
Heidelberg, Niels Kampmann,
c.1925–8

The Swiss designer Jan Tschichold
reproduced this poster in his
landmark treatise, *Die neue
Typographie* (1928). It demonstrates
some of his basic principles of layout
and book design, such as asymmetry,
contrast in type size and lack of
margins.

97
**Adolphe Jean-Marie Mouron
Cassandre** (1901–1968),
blad (book layout and design)
for the typeface *Bifur*
Paris, Deberny & Peignot, c.1925–30

Cassandre, better known for
his posters, designed several
typefaces for Deberny & Peignot,
an eminent French type foundry.
This blad for *Bifur* uses cut-outs,
cellophane inserts and foil-coated
paper to emphasize the ultra-
modern design.

98 (OPPOSITE)
László Moholy-Nagy (1895–1946),
cover proof for the first issue of
die neue linie
Leipzig, Otto Beyer, 1929

Moholy-Nagy's Surrealist
photomontage for the cover of
the first issue of *die neue linie*, sent
to the Library in 1936, typifies the
design ethos of a magazine that was
new in both content and design.
Colour proofs provided students
with examples of a particular stage
in the printing process.

erscheinungsort: berlin

die neue linie

september

1929

moholy-nagy

heft 1 · september 1929 · preis 90 pfg · verlag otto beyer · leipzig / berlin

99
Ausstellung Walter Gropius: Zeichnungen, Fotos, Modelle: in der ständigen Bauwelt-Musterschau, designed by László Moholy-Nagy (1895–1946), text by Max Osborn (1870–1946) (Berlin: Schinkelsaal des Architektenhauses, 1930)

Using Constructivist approaches to typography and layout, Moholy-Nagy conveys a sense of the new functionalism in architecture and the applied arts. This exhibition catalogue celebrates the work of Walter Gropius.

100
Interlaken, Switzerland, designed by Herbert Matter (1907–1984) and C.A. Weiland (Interlaken: O. Schlaefli, c.1935)

Travel was one of the 15 sections in the Library's exhibition of *Modern Commercial Typography*, displayed in late 1936. Swiss resorts needed to satisfy the burgeoning interest in outdoor activities and health that was a central preoccupation of modernism. Herbert Matter's dynamic 'Foto-graphik' technique aptly portrays Interlaken as a fresh and vibrant destination.

101
Serge Chermayeff (1900–1996), *Colours: Decoration of Today No. 3* (London: Nobel Chemical Finishes, 1936)

The modernist architect Serge Chermayeff wrote, illustrated and designed this brochure for a paint company. It incorporates techniques characteristic of the 1930s, such as spiral binding and colour printing on plastic (with blocks of colour adding layers of colour to the image below). The company thus appeared as forward thinking and in touch with the latest technologies.

102
Eric Newton (1893–1965),
An Approach to Art, designed by
Blair Hughes-Stanton (1902–1981)
(London: British Broadcasting
Corporation, 1935)

Newton's radio lectures for the
BBC were among a number of
initiatives to make consumer
taste more sympathetic to modern
design. The surreal juxtaposition
of images in Hughes-Stanton's
wood engraving shows that British
modernism did not entirely reject
traditional arts and crafts.

103
'**Three show-cards . . . Centre,
for Shell Lubricating Oil,
designer: E. McKnight Kauffer**',
in *Modern Publicity*, 1937–8
(London: The Studio Ltd, 1938)

McKnight Kauffer's mechanistic
design contrasts with the
illustrative but still modernist
landscapes on these pages.
They all convey Shell-Mex's
corporate patronage of modern
artists and significant designers.
The periodical *Modern Publicity*
regularly highlighted work of
this kind in its annual review.

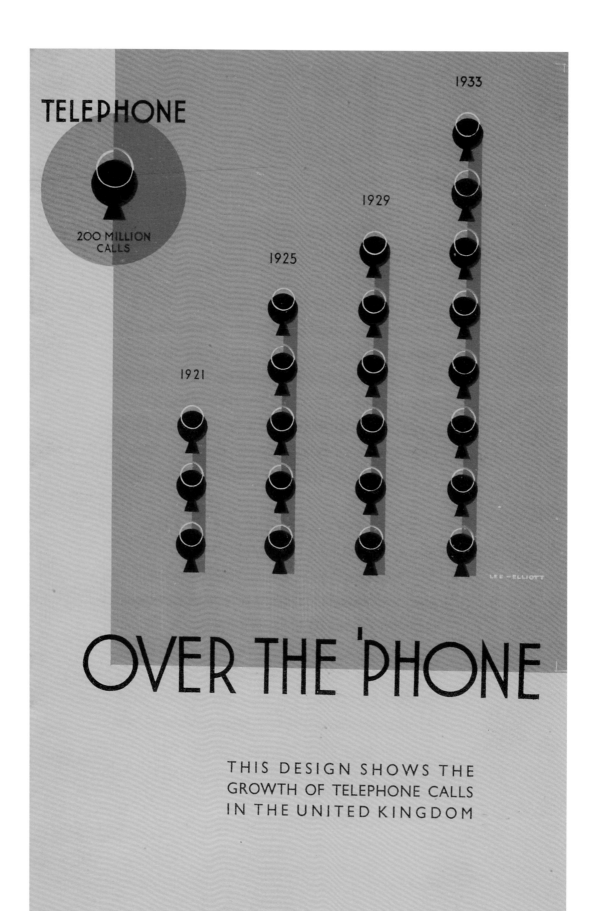

104 (OPPOSITE)
Great Britain Post Office,
Over the Phone, designed by
Theyre Lee-Elliott (1903–1988)
(London: GPO, 1935)

105 (RIGHT)
Great Britain Post Office,
Extension, designed by G.R. Morris
(London: GPO, c.1936)

106 (BELOW)
Great Britain Post Office,
Night Mail: The Travelling Post Office,
designed by Pat Keely (d.1970)
(London: GPO, 1939)

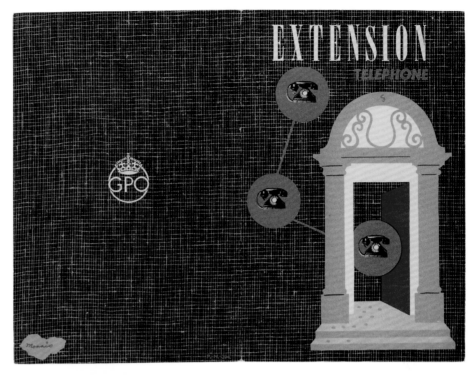

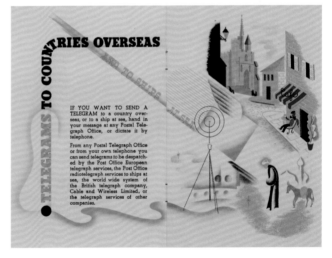

107 (ABOVE)
Great Britain Post Office,
Overseas Telegrams, designed
by London Art Service Ltd
(London: GPO, 1939)

Sir Stephen Tallents (1884–1958),
Public Relations Officer at the
General Post Office from 1933,
was responsible for re-designing
the GPO's image as a leader in
communications technology.
Leaflets and posters promoting
the GPO exposed the public to a
range of modernist styles: Theyre
Lee-Elliott's diagrams were an
early form of making images
relay statistical information. Pat
Keely's striking images for the
Night Mail leaflet echo the iconic
promotional film of the same title
(with its words by W.H. Auden
and music by Benjamin Britten).
Tallents ensured that designers'
names appeared on their works.

6
The Fashion Archive

From its inception the Library collected works on costume, but only occasionally did these include works about contemporary fashion. The section on 'Costume, Manners and Customs' in the catalogue of the Library published in 1855 referred almost entirely to historical costume, from classical antiquity to the medieval and early modern periods. There were works on ecclesiastical vestments, professional attire, military uniforms, royal robes and the dress of farmers and peasants, but none that gave guidance for contemporary fashions. The styles of the day were represented solely by issues of the *Petit courrier des dames* (Paris, 1833–7). Although a heading 'Fashions' did appear in the Library catalogue, it referred only to the *Miroir de la mode* of 1803. Fashion was similarly absent from the *List of Works on Costume* in the National Art Library of 1881, a work more useful to painters of historical subjects than followers of fashion. A work like *How To Dress on £15 a Year as a Lady – By a Lady* (London, 1873) joined the Library only in the twentieth century; *The Art of Dress* (1879) by Mrs H.R. Haweis, however, was acquired on publication, since it captured the Aesthetic Movement's interest in new principles of dress.

On the other hand, there was a substantial fashion industry in Britain, and technical works on this trade came to the Library as a matter of course. Tailoring and dressmaking were good professions for young men and women, and the Library provided manuals and pattern books for students and apprentices, as it did for a wide range of other trades. Works on associated skills such as millinery, lacework, embroidery and crochet were also extensively collected. Books on technique were not restricted to current publications; Juan de Alcega's *Libro de geometria* (Madrid, 1589), the oldest known book on garment cutting in the world, was bought in 1879.

By the twentieth century the invention of paper patterns by manufacturers such as Ebenezer Butterick and the availability of home sewing machines meant that even those on a modest income could follow trends. With industrial methods of manufacturing clothing and the corresponding availability of cheaper clothes, manufacturers and retailers began to publish stylish, eye-catching publicity material to advertise their designs. As part of its interest in trade literature, the National Art Library received promotional material from the whole spectrum of the clothing industry, which today provides a visual record of changing styles.

Systematic engagement with the fashion industry began in the V&A after 1945. By the time of the first exhibitions devoted to contemporary fashion – *A Lady of Fashion* in 1960 and above all *Fashion: An Anthology* organized with Cecil Beaton (1904–1980) in 1971 – the Library had a substantial base of works on fashion that developed with the Museum's initiatives to play a part in creating and celebrating contemporary fashion. Significant early catalogues by haute couture designers had been acquired, such as Paul Poiret's highly inventive and self-consciously collectable *Les choses de Paul Poiret vues par Georges Lepape* (Paris, 1911), which, along with *Les robes de Paul Poiret racontées par Paul Iribe* (Paris, 1908), inaugurated de luxe fashion publishing in an Art Deco style. More recently, luxury fashion brands such as Yohji Yamamoto, Gianni Versace and Prada have continued to commission work by an impressive range of influential fashion image-makers to produce artful, limited-edition, seasonal catalogues, which, like their predecessors, have often acquired a cult status of their own.

Fashion periodicals are a crucial source in plotting changes in fashion each season. Some were relatively short-lived and evocative of an era (for example, *Nova*, 1965–75), while others have remained behemoths of style reportage for more than a century (these include *Vogue* and *Harper's Bazaar*) and venture on into the digital age. Periodicals also provide a rich visual resource of work by artists, photographers and illustrators of the stature of Richard Avedon and René Gruau. Original photographs and illustrations of their work can be seen among the Word and Image Department's collections of prints, drawings, photographs and designs, while whole archive-groups of designers, suppliers and businesses who operated in the British fashion industry are held in the V&A's Archive of Art and Design (founded in 1978), those of Biba (fashion retailer and department store) and John French (fashion photographer) among them.

Conceptual designer brands have moved beyond the realms of conventional fashion promotion to produce creative publications that resemble book art, for example, Comme des Garçon's avant-garde magazine *Six* (1988–91). Fashion enthusiasts continue to enjoy inventive and inspiring projects such as Stephen Gan's shape-shifting artists' periodical *Visionaire* (1991–), while an artist's book such as Marshall Weber's *The Catalog* (1997) provides a fittingly barbed commentary on some of the extravagant mores of the fashion industry.

108
Georges Lepape (1887–1971),
Les choses de Paul Poiret vues par Georges Lepape (Paris: Pour Paul Poiret, 1911)

Georges Lepape used simple shapes and bold, flat areas of colour to illustrate Poiret's couture collection of 1911. The oriental style of Poiret's dress designs are said to have been influenced by the collections of Indian costume and Persian miniatures that he had seen in the V&A.

109
Janine Aghion,
The Essence of the Mode of the Day (Paris: La Belle Edition, 1920)

This English edition of a de luxe album of drawings was testament to the success of the modern 'Art Deco' style of fashion illustration. The illustrations depict ladies of leisure wearing the latest fashions, but they do not represent named couture models.

THE MOD-
ERN EMPIRE

AT VIONNET
A NEW
SILHOU-
ETTE
PURE
AS
A

CLASSIC
URN MOULDED
TIGHT OVER
THE POITRINE.
PALE
FLESH-PINK
CREPE
CUT VERY LOW
WITH A
BLAZING JEWEL
AT THE POINT
OF
DECOLLETAGE.
IN SHORT A
GLORIFIED
NIGHTGOWN
CLINGING
TO THE
FIGURE
BUT
CUT
WITH
SUCH
SKILL
THAT
IT IS A
GRANDE TOILETTE

VIONNET from MAISON ARTHUR

Man Ray

32

A FIGURE
MOULDED
IN
GOLD
LAME
AND
NOW
FOR
THE

FIRST TIME
AN EMPIRE
DRESS
BECOMES
REALLY
WEARABLE
FOR THE FULNESS
IS STITCHED
TO FALL
FLAT AND SLIM
OVER THE HIPS
THE SILHOUETTE
IS YOUNG. THE
DECOLLETAGE
IS TREATED
MOST BEAUTI-
FULLY
THIS IS
VIONNET'S
GREAT-
EST
DRESS..
A HUSH
FELL
WHEN IT
PASSED IN
THE COLLECTION..

Man Ray

VIONNET from EVA LUTYENS

33

110
Photograph by Man Ray
(1890–1976) in *Harper's Bazaar*,
British edition, October 1937

Successive editors of *Harper's Bazaar*,
like Carmel Snow and later Diana
Vreeland, employed avant-garde
artists to ensure that the magazine
stayed at the forefront of taste
and style. Exhibitions in London
and New York in 1936 had sparked
international interest in Surrealism.

113 (OPPOSITE)
British Nylon Spinners Ltd,
*British Nylon in International Haute
Couture* (Pontypool, 1958)

Nylon, until then an unfashionable
product developed for toothbrush
bristles and hosiery, was promoted
to replace traditional fabrics used
for couture garments. The best
designers, photographers and models
were employed.

111

Ministry of Information,
Make Do and Mend (London, 1943)

War-torn Britain had little inclination
to worry about fashion. Warm,
serviceable clothing and making
the best of whatever was to hand
were the priorities. The Government
offered assistance by publishing
this guide to reusing and recycling
garments and household materials.

112

Moss Bros, *Some Sartorial
Consequences of the Second World War*
(London, 1946)

Even before the Second World War,
this high-end retailer produced
a series of light-hearted books to
amuse its customers. The format
here allows the reader to mix and
match outfits, thereby creating new
looks without the expense of buying
new clothes.

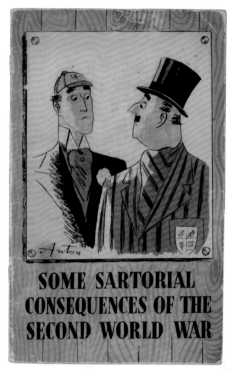

NORMAN HARTNELL *clouds of nylon net make this classic ball gown, embroidered with spray design in sequins and brilliants.*

GRES *slim afternoon dress in grey nylon and alpaca woven with fine irregular stripings to create surface interest.*

114 (OPPOSITE)
John French (1907–1966),
photograph of Mary Quant designs,
1962 (acquired 1979)

Jean Shrimpton (b.1942) and
Celia Hammond (b.c.1943) model
Mary Quant's designs for a flannel
knickerbocker suit and day dress.
Fashion photographer John French
pioneered a technique using natural
light and low contrast, which made
reproduction in newspapers easier
than conventional images.

115
Mary Quant (b.1934),
Quant by Quant (London, 1966)

Mary Quant was successful
enough at the age of 32 to write her
autobiography, in a book with a
cover photograph by David Bailey
(b.1938). She was also the right age to
wear the clothes she designed, have
a dramatic hairstyle (the Quant cut)
by Vidal Sassoon (1928–2012) and
market her own range of make-up.

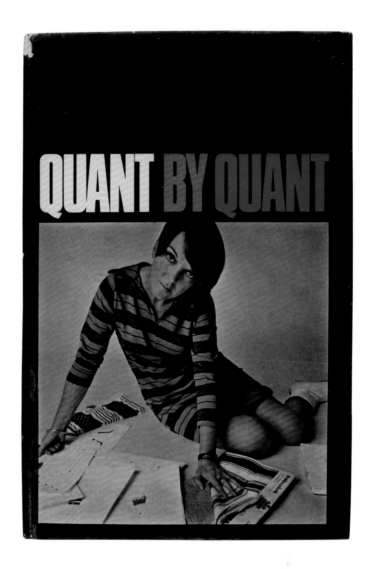

116

**Mail-order catalogue produced
by Biba**, 1968

In 1968 the Biba mail-order business
was relaunched through a series of
newly designed, slimline catalogues
that could fit through a standard
letterbox. Each catalogue presented
only eight garments and 'had the
atmosphere of a magazine editorial',
an idea inspired by the founder,
Barbara Hulanicki (b.1936).
Six catalogues were produced.
The mail-order department was
closed in the summer of 1969.

117

Punk Fanzines, *Sunday Mirra*
and *Toxic Graffiti* (London, 1977)

Punk was characterized by torn
clothing, Mohican haircuts, anarchy
and anti-establishment music.
Disaffected youth provided fertile
ground for home-grown publications
produced by photocopies; they
were non-professional and non-
profit making, being passed from
hand to hand. The fashions were
widely adopted, to the extent
that they were subsequently
appropriated by couture designers.

118

Nick Knight (b.1958),
cover photograph for Yohji Yamamoto
womenswear catalogue for Autumn
1986 (Tokyo, 1986)

This modern ensemble of a long
black coat by Yohji Yamamoto
playfully incorporates an 1880s-
style bustle in red tulle. This
nod to historicism is gleefully
acknowledged by Nick Knight's
striking photograph in silhouette,
resembling an exotic bird of paradise.

120
Bruce Weber (b.1946),
photo spread for Gianni Versace
menswear catalogue for Autumn
1995, no. 29 (Milan, 1995)

Gianni Versace's homoerotic
advertising campaigns were
enormously influential in the 1990s
fashion industry. Bruce Weber's
photographs for the menswear
catalogue for Autumn 1995 capture
the humour and theatricality yet
sophistication and quality of the
Versace brand.

121

Martin Margiela (b.1977), *(9/4/1615),*
exhibition catalogue for Museum
Boijmans Van Beuningen
(Rotterdam, 1997)

Published on the occasion of
the brand's first 'solo' exhibition
at the Museum Boijmans Van
Beuningen in Rotterdam, this
exhibition catalogue has a
deliberate artisanal quality and
presents a series of Margiela
ensembles using photocollages
in a familiar monochrome palette.

122

Marshall Weber (b.1960),
The Catalog (New York: AYP, 1997)

The artist Marshall Weber takes
the fashion mail-order catalogue
as a source of inspiration for
this artist's book. Found images
from real catalogues have been
cut up and reworked to produce
photocollages of models in
disconcerting and irreverent poses.

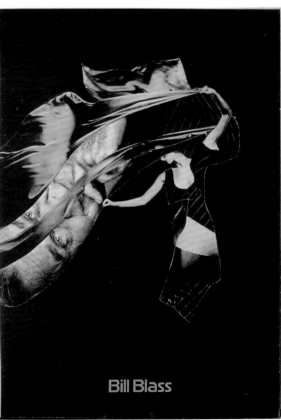

Founded in 1991, *Visionaire* describes
itself as 'a multi-format album of
fashion and art'. Published three
times a year, each issue explores a
different theme. This arresting image
of the model Kate Moss swinging to
and fro is a lenticular photograph by
Nick Knight (b.1958) and forms the
front and back cover of issue no. 27,
on the theme of movement.

In recent years, Rem Koolhaas's
Office for Metropolitan Architecture
(OMA/AMO) think tank has been
collaborating with the fashion
label Prada on many projects
from designing catwalk shows to
producing a series of look books for
their seasonal collections. The latter
are presented like a series of movie
stills in a virtual blend of fashion
and architecture.

7
Modern Artists and the Book

'The century of artists' books' (so-called by the historian and artist Johanna Drucker) began in 1900 with *Parallèlement*, the first book issued by Ambroise Vollard, the Paris art dealer. Not immediately successful in the existing bibliophile market, its quality became recognized as Vollard pursued his venture (more than 40 books by the time of his death in 1939), and as others came forward to publish, in the same mould, classic or modern literary texts with illustrations reproduced as original prints by established or up-and-coming artists.

A different lineage began with the American artist Edward Ruscha's self-published photo book *26 Gasoline Stations* (1963), and near-contemporary works by Sol LeWitt and Dieter Roth, although their aspects of artist-initiated control and distribution had characterized publications from earlier art movements too.

Around 1900 the graphic arts were boosted by commercial and advertising opportunities, technology and new aesthetics. Artists of all styles and movements found the space of the page an exhilarating medium and have been inspired by it ever since, whether in luxury commissions, jobbing work or to disseminate their own work and ideas cheaply. This section is broadly divided between works in the *livre d'artiste* tradition and artist-led publications, with Picasso's anti-Franco cartoons a hinge between the two.

Among the dealers, Vollard associated with post-Impressionist artists influenced by Cézanne; Kahnweiler championed Cubism, and sought out new writers. Jeanne Bucher's gallery published the Surrealist artists she showed, using standard trade production, the artists taking the lead. Other dealers participating occasionally included Gerald Cramer (whose *A toute épreuve*, 1958, with the prolific Miró was a triumph) and E.W. Kornfeld: he lent his imprint to Walasse Ting's *1¢ life* (1964), edited (and substantially funded) by Sam Francis, whom Kornfeld represented. In this book CoBrA members rubbed shoulders with Abstract Expressionists and Pop artists. (Situationists self-published, being too contrary to cooperate.) Tériade, like Albert Skira, was a publisher but not a dealer, supporting artists not only with books but also with his journal *Verve* (1937–60).

These examples inspired printmakers and publishers in the 1960s, when new techniques, especially screen printing, were taken up. In London, Editions Alecto was initially founded in 1960–62 solely to sell prints, but (after the American examples

ULAE and Tamarind) became highly important in enabling major work by artists both established (Paolozzi) and new (Hockney), especially in portfolio series.

Even books clearly initiated and controlled by artists may rely on financial, technical and even creative design input from behind the scenes. The Cologne-based bookseller and art publisher Walther König produced both editions of *Side by Side* (1972, 2012) for Gilbert & George, while the printing expertise of Hansjörg Mayer, from Stuttgart, has been crucial not only to Dieter Roth's lifelong book production but also to the success of Tom Phillips's now mass-market *Humument* (1985 and later).

The *Humument* originated in the hand 'alteration' of an existing book, using painting, drawing and collage to expose unintended subtexts through erasure. *The Book of Nails* (1992) manifests an extreme example of this approach, suppressing the text utterly. Is it fanciful to classify the bookbinding of Philip Smith as a form of alteration? In technical innovation and creative ambition he has led his craft towards a condition of equality with the text. All these exceed the normal limits of the page, crossing into what Drucker called 'the conceptual space in which artists' books operate'.

Finally Susan kae Grant's book, for all its physicality, reminds us that language too, 'a proper name', is sometimes vital to rendering experience, while Ian Hamilton Finlay's poster poem synchronizes word and image.

125 (OPPOSITE, ABOVE)
Pierre Bonnard (1867–1947),
Parallèlement, poems by Paul Verlaine
(Paris: Ambroise Vollard, 1900)
Lithographs printed by Auguste Clot,
wood engravings cut by T. Beltrand,
text printed at the Imprimerie
nationale

Bonnard spent two years completing
109 lithographs, all printed in 'rose
sanguine'. His method of making
crayon and graphite sketches
directly on page proofs of the printed
text imbued them with a loose
extemporized immediacy fitting
the sensuous poetry.

126 (OPPOSITE, BELOW)
Pablo Picasso (1881–1973),
Le chant des morts, poems by Pierre
Reverdy (Paris: Tériade, 1948)
Lithographs printed by Mourlot
Frères, text printed by Draeger Frères

Relentlessly original, Picasso
floods Reverdy's handwritten
texts with readerly markings
in scarlet throughout.

ALLÉGORIE.

Un très vieux temple antique s'écroulant
Sur le sommet indécis d'un mont jaune,
Ainsi qu'un roi déchu pleurant son trône
Se mire, pâle, au tain d'un fleuve lent;

Grâce endormie & regard somnolent,
Une naïade âgée, auprès d'un aulne,
Avec un brin de saule agace un faune
Qui lui sourit, bucolique & galant.

Sujet naïf & fade qui m'attriste,
Dis, quel poète entre tous les artistes,
Quel ouvrier morose t'opéra,

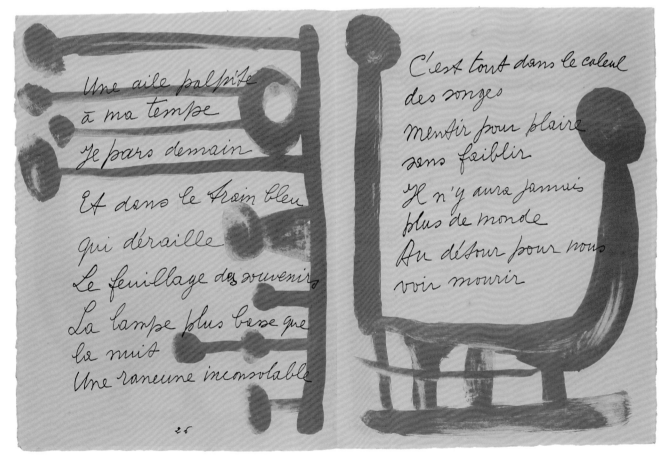

Une aile palpite
à ma tempe
Je pars demain
Et dans le train bleu
qui déraille
Le feuillage des souvenirs
La lampe plus basse que
la nuit
Une rancune inconsolable

25

C'est tout dans le couleur
des songes
Mentir pour plaire
sens faiblir
Il n'y aura jamais
plus de monde
Au détour pour nous
voir mourir

Des murs
Sont laids.

Ils n'y auront pas mis
Du leur.

Faits pour cacher,
Pour empêcher,

Amidonnés parfois
De tessons de bouteilles.

— Ils n'arrêteront pas
Les foules du triomphe.

atmosphère de mon pays — mais, Seigneur, quand on est
pauvre et né avec quelque dignité, on est sous la coupe de
la Douleur même si on la maudit.

On disait mort l'Oiseau-Phénix,
Mais nuit et jour chante-t-il pas encore
Au cœur du captif ?

On répétait à satiété : les positivistes l'ont tué. Mais s'il
meurt, Oncle Sam, chez les riches matérialistes, il ressus-
cite chez ceux-là qui sont dépouillés.

A l'oiseau bleu
Crève les yeux,
Il chantera mieux.

Quand on parle tant de règle et pour les écoliers qu'on
veut le meilleur guide-âne, c'est qu'elle est vaine et bien
médiocre en fait, cette loi, cette règle qu'aux belles époques
on suit d'instinct sans tant en parler.

Le génie est un crime, chante ce matin
Certain critique arbitraire et mondain.

Mais bien que rien ne soit nouveau sous le soleil,
Jésus peut toujours ressusciter en tout cœur bien né, si
tu as chance, Tristes Os, de souhaiter voir naître quelque
beauté en ce monde qui sue l'ennui et sent la mort, si le
génie industrieux de quelque bienheureux fou ne nous
réjouit enfin le cœur de temps à autre.

36

127 (OPPOSITE, ABOVE)
Jean Dubuffet (1901–1985),
Les murs, poems by Eugène Guillevic
(Paris: Editions du Livre, 1950)
Lithographs printed by Mourlot
Frères, text printed by Joseph Zichieri

With the recurring 'wall' motif,
Guillevic's poem sequence addresses
post-war themes of alienation and
decrepitude. Dubuffet responded
to his invitation with prints
exploiting all the tonal possibilities
of lithography, evoking crumbling
masonry in a decaying urbanscape.

128 (OPPOSITE, BELOW)
Georges Braque (1882–1963),
Théogonie, text by Hesiod
(Paris: Maeght, 1955)
Etchings printed by
Fequet et Baudier

Originally commissioned by
Vollard and realized after his
death by Maeght, this book's
classical text was printed in
Greek, with Braque's Cubist
but rounded forms, influenced
by Greek vase illustration,
complementing its typography.

129
Georges Rouault (1871–1958),
Cirque de l'etoile filante (Paris: Ambroise
Vollard, 1938)
Engravings printed by Roger
Lacourière, wood engravings cut by
Georges Aubert, text printed at Aux
deux ours

Rouault's lengthy text is illustrated
throughout with wood engravings
and intensely coloured aquatints.
Rose Adler (1890–1959) designed
the binding for the V&A (see p.48).

Joan Miró (1893–1983),
À toute épreuve, poems by Paul Eluard
(Geneva: Gerald Cramer, 1958)
Printed in Paris, woodcuts at the
Atelier Lacourière

Miró sought 'to make a book, not
merely to illustrate it', working
over ten years with Enric Tormo
(b.1919) to cut the blocks, drawing
inspiration from the medium itself,
emphasizing the wood grain and
its textures.

131 (OPPOSITE, ABOVE)
Mel Ramos (b.1935),
'America', from *1¢ Life*, poems by
Walasse Ting, edited by Sam Francis
(Berne: E.W. Kornfeld, 1964)
Printed in Paris, lithographs by
Maurice Beaudet, text by Georges
Girard

Twenty-eight artists contributed
a total of 62 lithographs to
accompany 61 of the Chinese
immigrant artist Ting's
freewheeling, uninhibited poems.

132 (OPPOSITE, BELOW)
David Hockney (b.1937),
Fourteen Poems, by C.P. Cavafy,
translated by Nikos Stangos and
Stephen Spender, with 12 etchings
by David Hockney (London:
Editions Alecto, 1966)

David Hockney's association with
Editions Alecto was highly successful
for both parties. The publication
of his second Alecto series, frank
and delicate etchings for Cavafy,
was noteworthy at a moment when
homosexuality was only just being
decriminalized in Britain.

PAUL ELUARD

A TOUTE ÉPREUVE

Gravures sur bois de
JOAN MIRÓ

GÉRALD CRAMER
Genève

AMERICA

brain made by IBM & FBI
stomach supported by A&P
and Horn & Hardart
love supported by Time & Life
tongue supported by
American Telephone & Telegraph
soul made by 7up
skin start with Max Factor
heart red as U.S. Steel

three thousand miles
blue sky wallpaper
salt lake city kitchen
new england green garden
florida warm bed
new york city shining mirror
big mountain walk, big river sing
big tree fly in california
green banana hang
under new moon in montana
sun spit out sweet candy
in north dakota
star turn big diamond in iowa

red american as pumpkin
black american as horse
yellow american as sunflower
white american as fat woman
fat woman cut pumpkin
put sunflower in corner
push horse in dark
pumpkin dead
sunflower sad
horse angry
fat woman afraid horse make love
she stay alone
with
a
gun

153

Two boys aged 23 or 24

He had been at the café from half past ten
expecting him soon to appear.
Midnight – he was still waiting.
One thirty; now the café was nearly empty.
He bored himself reading newspapers
mechanically. Of his miserable three shillings
only one remained; the rest he spent
on coffee and brandy while waiting for so long.
He had smoked up all his cigarettes.
He felt exhausted now by waiting. Because,
being alone for hours, disturbing thoughts
of having gone astray in his life began to gnaw at him.

But when he saw his friend come in, at once
fatigue, boredom and worries disappeared.

His friend brought unexpected news.
He had won sixty pounds at the casino.

Their handsome faces, superb youth,
the sensual love they felt for one another,
were now refreshed, renewed, invigorated
by the sixty pounds from the casino.

And full of joy and strength, beauty and emotion,
they went – not to the houses of their decent families
(where they were now unwanted anyway)
but to a very special place they knew
of ill repute. They took a bedroom there
ordered expensive drinks and went on drinking.

And when the expensive drinks were finished,
when it was nearly dawn,
content, they gave themselves to love.

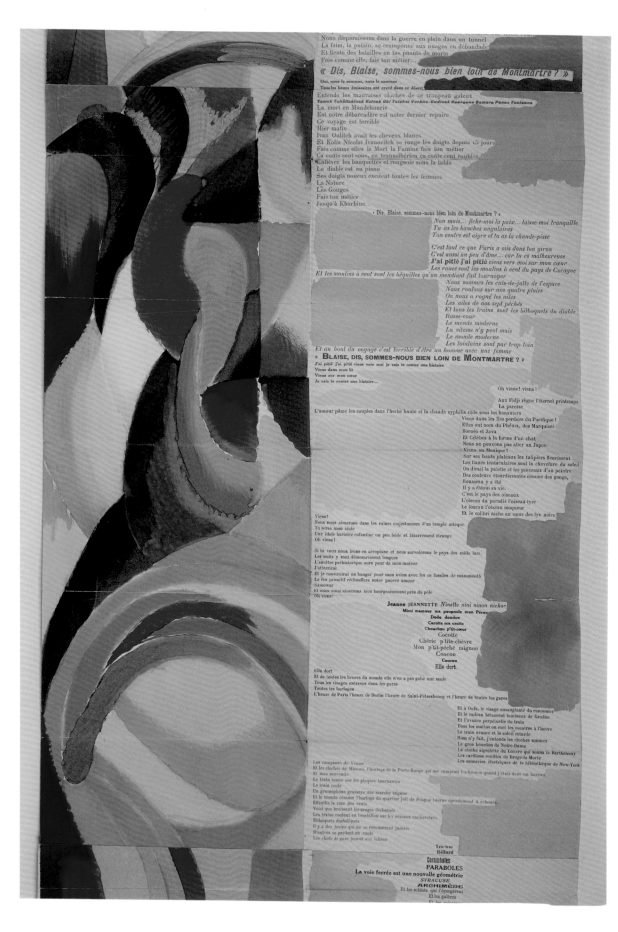

133
Blaise Cendrars (1887–1961)
and Sonia Delaunay (1885–1979),
*La prose du Transsibérien et de la petite
Jehanne de France* (Paris: Editions
des hommes nouveaux, 1913)
Letterpress, gouache and watercolour
on paper

This outsize poem (2 m. long) with
'simultaneous' colours was issued
folded like a railway map, fitting
its subject. Nothing better evokes
the cultural fertility of early 20th-
century Paris than this exhilarating
collaboration between Cendrars,
a Swiss-born poet (and here publisher),
and the Russian artist Delaunay.

134
Pablo Picasso (1881–1973),
Sueño y mentira de Franco (Paris, 1937)
Etchings printed by Roger Lacourière

With this pair of anti-Franco cartoon
strips and a Surrealist-style prose
poem, Picasso conceived a total work
of word and image, more accessible
and propagandistic than the painting
Guernica (1937), with which it shares
its indignation and some images.

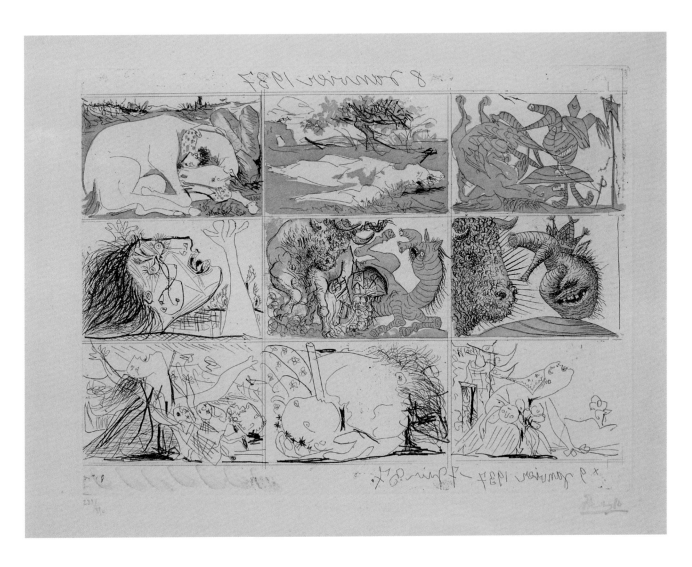

But the advance of the human intellect has not lain solely in the realm of natural science and what things I have seen there, excuse me, not many can do because of their bulk and because of their lack of retention of breath below the floor of hell.

We now enter the world of punishment, and the airframe makes it apparent that the design of each of these systems proves their need to assert their sexual superiority, . . . to which the eyes are exposed.
Under these conditions the Pukinje phenomenon does not occur.

Launching and airborne launcher design will be considered in detail in later chapters.
Honour, side by side, each pronounce the soft balsam - a lovely luminous transparancy.

To insure doubly against enlarged pores, however, Madame Rubinstein conceived a curtain.

Where one sister electrifies (they of all ages and conditions)
A third of them would be selling something in the line of food or drink - soda water, mineral waters from the Jade.

She would be standing with five men sitting behind her. She does not talk at them, as an Englishwoman might, about there being no gentlemen present.

R. P. 137 a . . . this marvellous mass wears a navy-blue skimmy knit dress, She does haul out her superb sapphire rings, we notice.

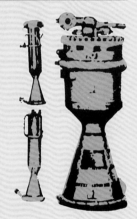

135 (OPPOSITE)

Eduardo Paolozzi (1924–2005),
Moonstrips Empire News, Vol. 1
(London: Editions Alecto, 1967)
Screen print
Given by Sir Eduardo Paolozzi

This is one of a series of magnificent
portfolios that Paolozzi was able to
achieve through his collaboration
with the Kelpra print studio. It is not
a bound book, but has many leaves of
text, presented in a pink acrylic box.

136

Max Ernst (1891–1976),
*Une semaine de bonté; ou, les sept
éléments capitaux: roman* (Paris:
Editions Jeanne Bucher, 1934)
Printed by Georges Duval
Given by Harry Fischer

In collage, the Surrealist theory
of chance encounters is taken
to the level of the part-object
or image, appropriated from an
existing context. A pioneer of the
technique, Ernst derived his scraps
from magazines, romantic novels,
pornography and trade catalogues.

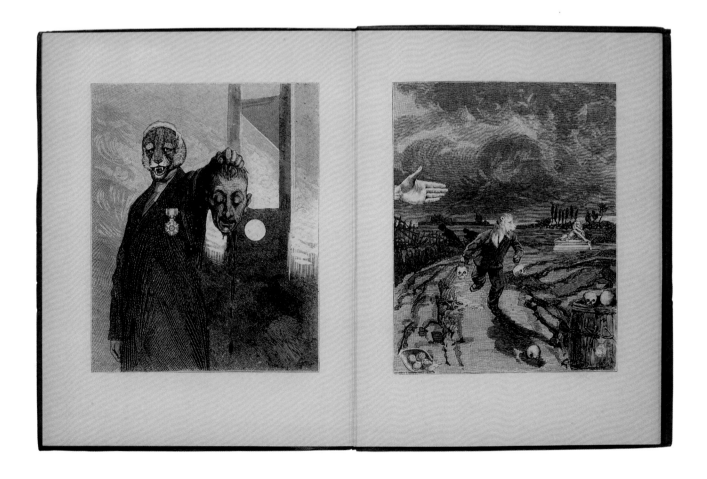

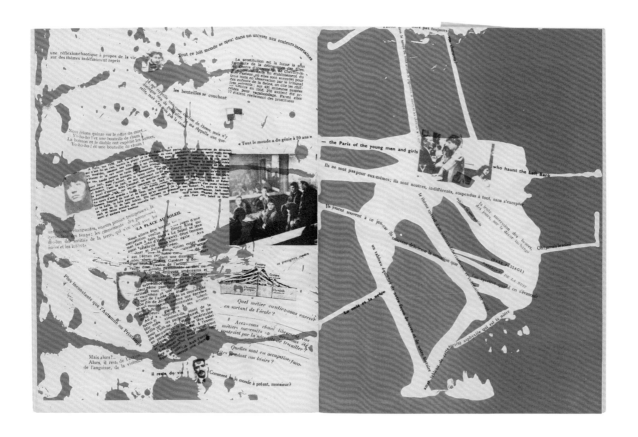

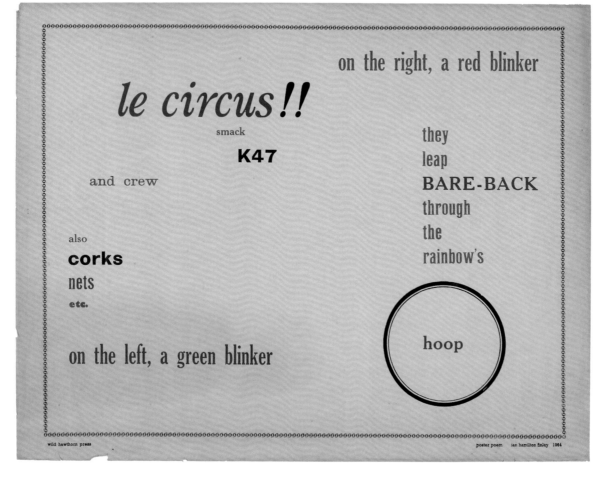

137 (OPPOSITE, ABOVE)
Guy Debord (1931–1994)
and **Asger Jorn** (1914–1973),
Mémoires (Copenhagen: L'Internationale
situationniste, 1959)
Printed by Permild & Rosengreen

This second book by two Situationist
founders obliquely treats Debord's
earlier dealings with the *Lettriste*
movement, in montages of snippets
and clippings, splattered Jackson
Pollock-style with acid colours. The
book-jacket of sandpaper symbolizes
less the abrasive radicalism of these
groups than the frictions among them.

138 (OPPOSITE, BELOW)
Ian Hamilton Finlay (1925–2006),
Poster Poem (Edinburgh: Wild
Hawthorn Press, 1964)
Screen print

An Orkney fishing boat ('smack'),
registered at Kirkwall, 'K47',
festooned with 'corks / nets / etc',
suggests a leaping circus horse.
Designed with reference to modernist
visual typography, the poster was
produced for Finlay's press by a
jobbing printer.

139
Edward Ruscha (b.1937),
Every Building on the Sunset Strip
(Los Angeles, 1966)
Edition of 1,000

Whereas Ruscha's earlier *26
Gasoline Stations* recorded single
points on a road trip, *Every Building
...* is a continuous panorama, 25
feet (7.5 m) long, accordion-folded.
Disorientatingly, the image is
printed as a border, one half always
upside down.

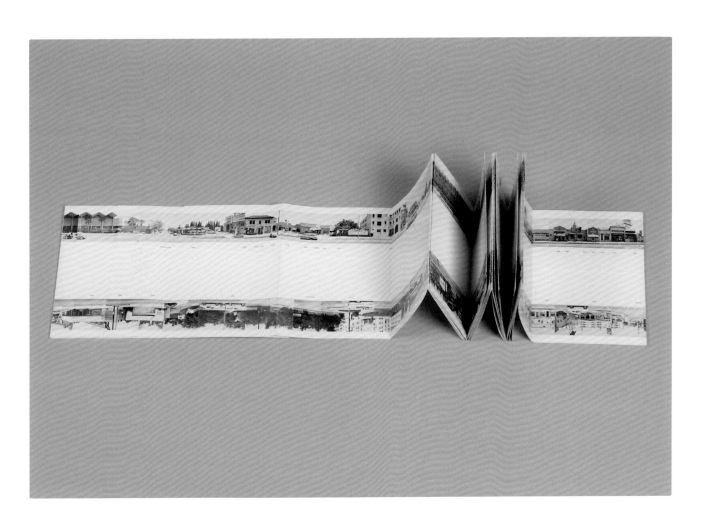

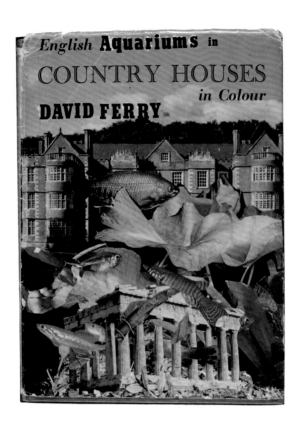

140
David Ferry (b.1957),
English Aquariums in Country Houses in Colour, 2010

This unique altered book is based on *English Country Houses in Colour*, photographs by A.F. Kersting (London: Batsford, 1958). Images of decorative fish are collaged onto the illustrations. A satire on the British stately home as genteel spectacle seems implied.

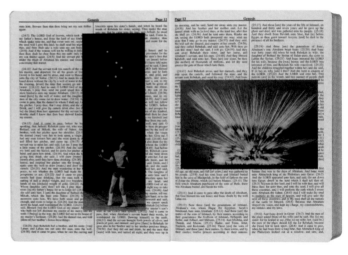

141
Adam Broomberg (b.1970) and Oliver Chanarin (b.1971), *Holy Bible*, 'His face to the earth' – Genesis 48:13; 'And it came to pass' – Genesis 24:16 (London: Mack; Archive of Modern Conflict, 2013)

An edition of the Bible overprinted with incongruous and disturbing images and underlinings. The Archive of Modern Conflict publishes artists' photo books, here drawing upon its large private collection of documentary and vernacular photographs.

142
Susan kae Grant (b.1954),
Giving Fear a Proper Name: Detroit
(Dallas, TX: Black Rose, 1984)

A letterpress-printed catalogue
of phobias in the physical form of
a personal photograph album, bound
in pink vinyl from a car factory.
Despite its handmade nature, this
book was published for multiple
distribution (an edition of 15).

143
Gilbert (b.1943) & George (b.1942),
Side by Side (London: Art for All,
and Cologne: Konig [*sic*] Brothers, 1972)

Attractively bound in marbled
cloth, three texts by the artists
are accompanied by photographs
depicting them in rural and urban
settings. A reissue by Enitharmon
Press in 2012 faithfully reproduced
the original production values.

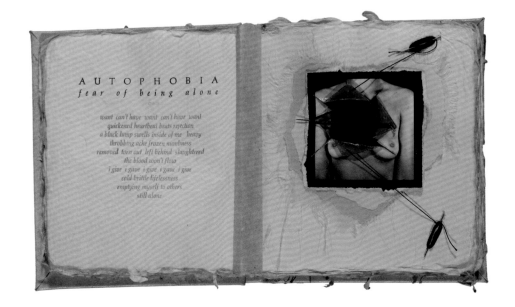

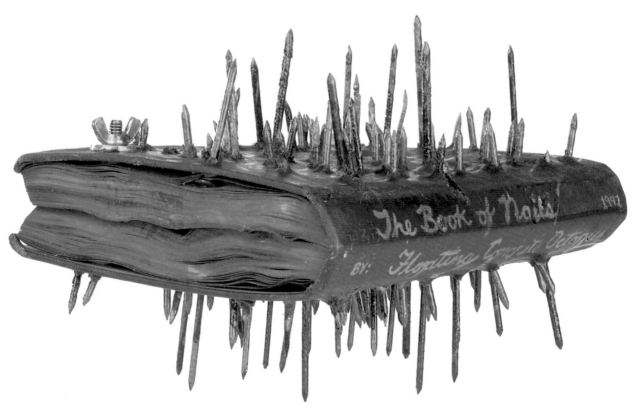

144 (OPPOSITE, ABOVE)
Philip Smith (b.1928),
'Book Wall' vol.3 from a series of five
bindings done in 1977 for *The English
Bible*, 5 vols (Hammersmith: Doves
Press, 1903–5)
Purchased with the assistance of the
National Art Collections Fund

The five volumes are magnificently
bound in Oasis goatskin, with stylized
depictions of the Creation worked
in 'maril', Smith's patent invention.
Pressed leather fragments create a
multicoloured matrix for paring,
and more conventional onlays.

145 (OPPOSITE, BELOW)
**Floating Concrete Octopus
(Miekal And** [b.1957] **and
Liz Was** [b.1956–2004]**),**
The Book of Nails (Madison, WI:
Xexoxial Endarchy, 1992)

Xexoxial Endarchy remains an
energetic collective, publishing
visual and experimental poetry
and art. For this unique
construction, a book about
Van Gogh was chosen, perhaps
invoking with humour the
cliché that suffering is the lot
of an artist.

146
Tom Phillips (b.1937),
Terrestrial and celestial *Humument*
globes, made by Sylvia Sumira
London, 1992
Plaster, wood and paper

The gores (sections) are collaged
from colour magazines. Language
derived from the *Humument*
project is pasted over the earth
and celestial spheres. Globes, often
part of a library's furniture, here
suggest, as did the philosopher
Derrida, that there is nothing
outside the text.

National Art Library at the V&A: Timeline

Major events, including a selection of exhibitions and publications

1837   Government School of Design opens in Somerset House, with a reference collection of 'casts, examples, books, &c' for students

1842   The Library allows students to borrow its 'works on art, useful knowledge and miscellaneous literature'

1851   *The Great Exhibition of the Works of Industry of All Nations*

1852   The Museum of Ornamental Art, and its library, opens to the public at Marlborough House

1855   The Library's first catalogue, arranged by subject, is published

1857   The Museum moves to South Kensington

1865   The Art Library becomes the National Art Library (NAL)

1866   Admission charges to the Library are abolished

1869   Alexander Dyce bequest, including Elizabethan and Jacobean literature, early Shakespeare publications, nineteenth-century literature

1870   First issue of the *Universal Catalogue of Books on Art*: 'Not only the books in the Library, but all … that could be required to make the Library perfect'

1875   *A List of Works on Pottery and Porcelain in the National Art Library*: the first subject bibliography issued by the Library

1876   John Forster bequest, including the Codex Forster (Leonardo da Vinci notebooks), Charles Dickens manuscripts, letters to Samuel Richardson, David Garrick correspondence, Jonathan Swift diaries and papers, nineteenth-century literature, autographs

1884   The NAL moves into the suite of purpose-built rooms that it still inhabits today

1901   *Loan Exhibition of Modern Illustration*

1902–3   George Reid gift of illuminated manuscripts

1909   Prints and drawings are transferred from the NAL to a separate department

Library exhibition gallery – 'Book Production Gallery' – opens

1916   *Shakespeare Tercentenary* (exhibition)

1932   *English Illustrated Children's Books* (exhibition)

1936–7   *Modern Commercial Typography* (exhibition)

1945   *Edward Johnston Memorial Exhibition*

1948   *Book Illustration by Picasso, Matisse, Rouault* (exhibition)

1949   *The Art of the Book-jacket* (exhibition)

1951   *British Books from Caxton to the Present*, Festival of Britain (exhibition)

1953   *Thomas Bewick Bicentenary* (exhibition)

1957   *Printed Books: A Short Introduction to Fine Typography* (book)

1964   *400 Years of English Handwriting* (exhibition)

1966   *Aubrey Beardsley* (exhibition)

1969   *Fine Illustration in Western European Printed Books* (book)

1970   Fernand and Anne Renier gift of more than 80,000 children's books to the NAL

Charles Dickens (exhibition)

1972   V&A Illustration Awards founded

1972–9   *Aspects of the Book* (exhibition series)

1973   Leslie Linder bequest of Beatrix Potter drawings, manuscripts, books, etc.

Victorian Books from the Library of the V&A (Europalia exhibition)

1974   *Byron* (exhibition)

1976   *The Art Press: Two Centuries of Art Magazines* (exhibition)

1978   Archive of Art and Design founded

Photography in Book Illustration (exhibition)

1979   *The Open and Closed Book* (exhibition)

1980   *The Universal Penman: A Survey of Western Calligraphy from Roman Times* (exhibition)

Berthold Wolpe (exhibition)

1981   *The History of the Illustrated Book* (book)

1982   *Reynolds Stone* (exhibition)

Illumination, Ancient and Modern (exhibition)

1983   *Islamic Bookbindings* (exhibition)

1985   *From Manet to Hockney: Modern Artists' Illustrated Books* (exhibition)

Beatrix Potter: The V&A Collections (exhibition)

1986   *Fable Books: 500 Years of Illustration* (exhibition)

1988   *A History of Children's Book Illustration* (book)

1990   NAL catalogue goes online

Rakoff Collection of Comics acquired

1992   V&A's historic archives made a department managed by the NAL; NAL takes responsibility for records management within the V&A

1996   Gift of Heinrich Robert Fischer Collection of early twentieth-century German publishing, including Expressionist, Dada and Bauhaus works and the *Entartete Kunst* inventory (1942) of works of art removed from German museums and art galleries by the Nazi government

1997   The Heritage Lottery Fund makes a grant of £1m for retrospective conversion of the book catalogue

2001   *The Art of the Book: From Medieval Manuscript to Graphic Novel* (book on NAL collections)

2003   Completion of the retrospective conversion of the NAL catalogue, funded by the Heritage Lottery Fund

Launch of the V&A Word and Image Department, reuniting prints, drawings, paintings and photographs collections with the Library and V&A Archive

2008   *Blood on Paper: The Art of the Book* (exhibition)

2010   *Small Books for the Common Man: A Descriptive Bibliography* (catalogue of the NAL's collection of 'chapbooks')

2011   *Western Illuminated Manuscripts: A Catalogue of Works in the National Art Library from the Eleventh to the Early Twentieth Century, with a Complete Account of the George Reid Collection* (book)

2015   *Word & Image: Art, Books and Design from the Victoria and Albert Museum's Library*, the first international touring exhibition drawn from NAL collections

Further reading

Chiara Barontini, *The National Art Library and its Buildings: From Somerset House to South Kensington* (London: NAL, 1995)

Joan M. Benedetti (ed.), *Art Museum Libraries and Librarianship* (Lanham, MD: Scarecrow Press /Art Libraries Society of North America, 2007)

James Bettley (ed.), *The Art of the Book: From Medieval Manuscript to Graphic Novel* (London: V&A, 2001)

Julius Bryant (ed.), *Art and Design for All: The Victoria and Albert Museum* (London: V&A, 2011)

Anthony Burton, *Vision and Accident: The Story of the Victoria and Albert Museum* (London: V&A, 1999)

Alice Grant, *Fashion Magazines from the 1890s to the 1980s: An Account Based on the Holdings of the National Art Library* (London: NAL, 1988)

Handbook of the Dyce and Forster Collections in the South Kensington Museum (London: Chapman and Hall for the Committee of Council on Education, 1880)

Elizabeth James, *The Victoria and Albert Museum: A Bibliography and Exhibition Catalogue 1852–1996* (London and Chicago: Fitzroy Dearborn and the V&A, 1998)

Edmund M.B. King, 'The South Kensington Museum Art Library: A Study of its Origins and Development until 1900', unpublished MA dissertation (University of London, 1975)

Anna Somers-Cocks, *The Victoria and Albert Museum: The Making of the Collections* (Leicester: Windward, 1980)

Rowan Watson, 'Educators, Collectors, Fragments and the "Illuminations" Collection at the Victoria and Albert Museum in the Nineteenth Century', in Linda L. Brownrigg and Margaret M. Smith (eds), *Interpreting and Collecting Fragments of Medieval Books* (Los Altos Hills, CA: Anderson Lovelace, and London: Red Gull Press, 2000), pp.21–46

Rowan Watson, *Western Illuminated Manuscripts: A Catalogue of Works in the National Art Library from the Eleventh to the Early Twentieth Century, with a Complete Account of the George Reid Collection*, photography by Paul Gardner, 3 vols (London: V&A, 2011)

Arthur Wheen, 'The Library of the Victoria and Albert Museum', in Raymond Irwin (ed.), *The Libraries of London* (London: Library Association, 1949), pp.48–54

Eva White, *The First Years of the National Art Library 1837–1853* (London: V&A, 1994)

Acknowledgements

This book would not have been possible without the generous support of Dr Susan Weber, Director of the Bard Graduate Center, New York City, together with support from the Iris Foundation.

The production of this book has been a collaborative effort by the staff of the National Art Library, with the help of colleagues in the Word and Image Department and other V&A curatorial departments. The catalogue sections were contributed by the following:

John Morton, Katy Temple and Alex Chanter (Resources for Art and Design Education)

Patrick Perratt, Emma Laws, Kirsten Pairpoint, Sally Williams and Frances Willis (Making Images: The Illustrator at Work)

Jonathan Hopson (Designers, Aesthetes and the 'Book Beautiful')

Anne Newport, Frances Willis and Joanna Brogan (The Impact of Photography)

Deborah Sutherland and Ruth Hibbard (Promoting Commercial Art: The Initiative of 1936)

Bernadette Archer and Diane Spaul (The Fashion Archive)

Elizabeth James and Nate Evuarherhe (Modern Artists and the Book)

Thanks are due to Philip Contos, Nazek Ghaddar, Nick Smith, Jill Raymond and Marc Ward. We are also grateful to the following for commenting on the text: Anthony Burton, Doug Dodds, Martin Flynn, Christopher Marsden and Gill Saunders.

This publication was produced to accompany an international touring exhibition, coordination of which was managed by Rosie Wanek and Olivia Oldroyd.

Abbreviations

AAD	Archive of Art and Design, Victoria and Albert Museum
EID	Department of Engraving, Illustration and Design, Victoria and Albert Museum
NAL	National Art Library, the library of the Victoria and Albert Museum
PDP	Department of Prints, Drawings and Paintings, Victoria and Albert Museum
WID	Word and Image Department, Victoria and Albert Museum

Notes

Julius Bryant: 'Word and Image'

1   The journal *Word & Image* was founded in 1985 as 'A Journal of Verbal/Visual Enquiry'. This range of topics is taken from the themes of its first and most recent issues.

2   The nine national collections in Word and Image are: the National Art Library; designs; the art of photography; posters and commercial graphics; computer art; British watercolours and drawings; portrait miniatures; pastels; John Constable. Word and Image also leads on the V&A's partnership with the Royal Institute of British Architects and organizes the annual V&A Illustration Awards.

3   T. Greenwood, *Free Public Libraries* (London, 1886); Thomas Kelly, *A History of Public Libraries in Great Britain 1845–1975* (London, 1977). The Public Libraries Act built on the Museums Act (1845).

4   Albert Predeek, *A History of Libraries in Great Britain and North America* (Chicago, 1947), p.94. New York Public Library was founded through the merger of several libraries in 1901 and opened in 1911.

5   T.W. Koch, *A Book of Carnegie Libraries* (New York, 1917); James W.P. Campbell, *The Library: A World History* (London, 2013), pp.234–7

6   Julius Bryant, 'Albertopolis: The German Sources of the Victoria and Albert Museum', in Julius Bryant (ed.), *Art and Design for All: The Victoria and Albert Museum* (London and Munich, 2011), pp.25–37

7   The art libraries at the National Gallery of Art in Washington DC (East Wing, 1978) and at the Getty Research Institute (mid-1980s) are more recent comparisons. For a list of art and design museums, see Bryant (cited note 6), p.267.

8   Oliver Impey and Arthur MacGregor (eds), *The Origins of Museums: The Cabinet of Curiosities in Sixteenth- and Seventeenth-century Europe* (Oxford, 1985); Hugh H. Genoway and Mary Anne Andrei (eds), *Museum Origins* (Walnut Creek, 2008)

9   Lionel Casson, *Libraries of the Ancient World* (New Haven, 2001)

10 The rival claims of librarians, curators and archivists as organizers of knowledge are discussed in Gerald Beasley, 'Curatorial Crossover: Building Library, Archives and Museum Collections', *RBM: A Journal of Rare Books, Manuscripts and Cultural Heritage* (Spring 2007), vol. 8, no. 1, pp.20–8.

11 *Report from Select Committee [of the House of Commons] on Arts and Manufactures: Together with the Minutes of Evidence, and Appendix* (London, 1835–6)

12 Ibid., pp.4, 5

13 These rooms are today the Courtauld Gallery. See Anthony Burton, 'The History of the Victoria and Albert Museum Library', lecture given to ASLIB members, 27 September 1974, typescript, National Art Library, V&A; Eva White, *From the School of Design to the Department of Practical Art: The First Years of the National Art Library 1837–1853* (London, 1994); Chiara Barontini, *The National Art Library and its Building* (London, 1995)

14 *Annual Report*, 1843–4

15 Walter R. Deverell (d.1853) became Secretary of the Government School of Design; his son Walter H. Deverell (1827–1854) trained under Rossetti as a Pre-Raphaelite painter and taught at the School of Design.

16 Walter R. Deverell, 'Report on the Lending Library', January 1846, printed in *Minutes of the Council of the Government School of Design*, 1 December 1846

17 *First Report of the Department of Practical Art* (1853), p.293, refers to the dismemberment of books as a 'former practice'.

18 Eva White, *The First Years of the National Art Library 1837–1853* (London, 1994), p.7

19 R.N. Wornum, 'The Government Schools of Design', *Art Journal* (January– February 1852), pp.16, 37–40. For Wornum, see *Oxford Dictionary of National Biography*, online edn: http://www.oxforddnb.

com/view/article/29978 (accessed 15 January 2014); Quentin Bell, *The Schools of Design* (London, 1963), pp.129–30, 215, 248; and David Robertson, *Sir Charles Eastlake and the Victorian Art World* (Princeton, 1978), p.140

20 Charles Heath Wilson (1809–1882), William Dyce's successor as Director of the School of Design from 1845, had served as part-time librarian.

21 R.N. Wornum, *Prospectus of the Library of the Section of Art at Marlborough House* (London, 1853), p.2

22 R.N. Wornum, *An Account of the Library of the Division of Art at Marlborough House* (London, 1855)

23 R.N. Wornum, *Catalogue of Ornamental Casts in the Possession of the Department, Third Division: The Renaissance Styles* (London, 1855)

24 Malcolm Baker, 'The Reproductive Continuum: Plaster Casts, Paper Mosaics and Photographs as Complementary Modes of Reproduction in the Nineteenth-century Museum', in Rune Frederiksen and Eckart Marchand (eds), *Plaster Casts: Making, Collecting and Displaying from Classical Antiquity to the Present*, vol. 18 of Hertmut Böhme et al. (eds), *Transformationen der Antike* (Berlin and New York: De Gruyter 2010), pp.485–500

25 Wornum (cited note 21), pp.2–4

26 William Bell Scott, *Autobiographical Notes*, ed. W. Pinto (London, 1892), vol. 1, p.156. Wornum's statuesque wife was the American stepdaughter of the classical scholar Professor George Long. They married in 1843. After her death he married his first cousin in 1861. On account of his white hair and beard, in later years he was affectionately known as 'old snowball'.

27 Anon., 'The Turner and Vernon Rooms, South Kensington Museum', *Illustrated London News* (4 February 1860), p.120. As well as the bequests, formerly shown at Marlborough House, Wornum hung a 'long gallery' devoted to the National Gallery's British School. These new, purpose-built, rooms on the north-

east side of the museum extend south from Room 94, where the Raphael cartoons hung from 1865 until 1939.

28 Henry Cole, 'The Functions of the Science and Art Department', in *Introductory Addresses on the Science and Art Department and the South Kensington Museum* (London, 1857), p.21

29 J.M. Crook, *The British Museum* (London, 1972); A. Esdaile, *The British Museum Library* (London, 1946)

30 Anthony Burton, *Vision and Accident: The Story of the Victoria and Albert Museum* (London, 1999), pp.68–9

31 For a diagrammatic evolution of the Museum's buildings, see Bryant (cited note 6), pp.34–5

32 J.C. Robinson, *Catalogue of the Art Library* (London, 1862), p.2. A first proof 'under revision' is dated 1861.

33 Elizabeth James, 'Publishing the Museum Collections', in Bryant (cited note 6), pp.186–7. Later publications included *Furniture* (1879), *Lace and Needlework* (1879), *Anatomy* (1880), *Glass* (1887) and *Ceramics* (1895)

34 Burton (cited note 30), pp.68–71

35 Alan Cole and Henrietta Cole, *Fifty Years of Public Works of Sir Henry Cole, KCB, Accounted for in his Deeds, Speeches and Writings*, 2 vols (London, 1884), vol. 1, p.345

36 Bryant (cited note 6), pp.197–207

37 *Universal Catalogue of Books on Art* (London, 1870), p. iv. Elizabeth Bonython and Anthony Burton, *The Great Exhibitor: The Life and Work of Henry Cole* (London, 2003), p.144. See also Anthony Burton, 'The Making of the Universal Catalogue of Books on Art (1870)', typescript of draft article, NAL (2002). In his 'Memorandum' on p. iii of the *Universal Catalogue*, Cole acknowledges that the idea 'is based on a suggestion of Mr Dilke's, made in the *Athenaeum* before 1851'.

38 Burton (cited note 30), p.89, note 123. Cole wrote in January 1866 to about 30 overseas scholars and 83 in Britain. See Bonython and Burton (cited note 37), p.238. At the British Museum Antonio Panizzi also asked

subject specialists to provide lists of desiderata.

39 *The First Proofs of the Universal Catalogue of Books on Art* (London, 1870), vol. 1, p. i

40 The term first appears in the Library's thirteenth Annual Report (1865), where R. Laskey is identified as 'Divisional Keeper of the National Art Library'. He is cited as 'Assistant Keeper of the Art Library' in 1863 and 1864.

41 The exhibition was *Works of Art of the Medieval, Renaissance and More Recent Periods*, drawn from British private collections.

42 Soden Smith appears in the fourteenth Annual Report (1866) as 'Provisional Librarian' and as Keeper the following year.

43 Anon., 'The Art Library at South Kensington', *The Builder* (9 October 1869), pp.799–801

44 *Art Pictorial & Industrial* (1870–1), vol. 1, p.198, cited in Burton (cited note 30), p.117

45 Barbara Morris, *Inspiration for Design* (London, 1986), pp.104–5

46 Twenty-second Annual Report (1885), pp.189, 298

47 John Physick, *The Victoria and Albert Museum: The History of its Building* (London, 1982), pp.172–6

48 Nikolaus Pevsner, *A History of Building Types* (London, 1976), pp.96–7

49 Burton (cited note 30), p.123

50 Mark Haworth-Booth, *Photography: An Independent Art: Photographs from the Victoria and Albert Museum* (London, 1997), pp.79–88

51 R.A. Rye, *The Libraries of London* (London, 1908), p.33; R.A. Rye, *The Students' Guide to the Libraries of London* (London, 1927), p.266

52 Arthur Wheen, 'The Library of the Victoria and Albert Museum', in Raymond Irwin (ed.), *The Libraries of London* (London, 1949), p.48

53 C.H. Gibbs-Smith, 'The Photographic Collection of the Victoria and Albert Museum', *Museums Journal* (April 1936), vol. 36, no. 1, pp.46–53. See also Anthony J. Hamber, 'A Higher Branch of the Art': *Photographing the Fine Arts in England 1839–1880* (Amsterdam, 1996), pp.393–452

54 Katia Mazzucco, 'Images on the Move: Some Notes on the Bibliothek Warburg Bildersammlung (Hamburg) and the Warburg Institute Photographic Collection (London)', *Art Libraries Journal* (2013), vol. 38, no. 4, pp.16–24

55 See Bryant (cited note 6), pp.154–61, cat. 100–2

56 Francis Haskell, *History and its Images* (New Haven and London, 1993), p.452. Haskell must be mistaken in stating, p.453, that Weale joined the Library staff in 1878.

57 Weale's teaching career was shortened by a jail sentence for thrashing a pupil.

58 Additions were made by cutting up the printed entries, pasting them into albums and inserting new references in between. This system continued for the subject catalogue until 1987.

59 Rowan Watson, 'Educators, Collectors, Fragments and the "Illuminations" Collection at the Victoria and Albert Museum in the Nineteenth Century', in Linda L. Brownrigg and Margaret M. Smith (eds), *Interpreting and Collecting Fragments of Medieval Books* (London, 2000), pp.37, 43–4

60 Weale also married a 16-year-old Irish girl, with whom he had 11 children. See H.P. Mitchell, 'The Late Mr W.H. James Weale', *Burlington Magazine* (1917), vol. 30, pp.241–3. See also Burton (cited note 30), pp.136–48, and Maurice W. Brockwell, 'W.H. James Weale: The Pioneer', *The Library* (1951), 5th series, vol. 6, pp.202–4

61 Mitchell (cited note 60), p.243

62 Anon., 'The Chronicle of Art – October', *The Magazine of Art* (1897), vol. 21, p.341

63 W.H.J. Weale, *Bookbindings and Rubbings of Bindings in the National Art Library, South Kensington Museum* (London, 1898)

64 R.A. Rye, *The Libraries of London*, 2nd edn (London, 1927), pp.267–9

65 The Circulation Department was newly created to take over from the National Art Library responsibility for loans to the regional art schools. In 1870 there were 2,313 prints, drawings and photographs out on loan to the Schools of Art.

66 Burton (cited note 30), pp.141–212

67 Anon., 'Obituary: Mr W.H. James Weale', *The Times* (28 April 1917), p.3

68 Anon., 'Mr G.H. Palmer', *The Times* (5 July 1945), p.7

69 A. van de Put, 'The Victoria and Albert Museum Library', *ASLIB Information* (December 1935), pp.2–3

70 Wheen was awarded the Military Medal with two bars. He was appointed Acting Keeper in 1939 and Keeper in 1945.

71 Kenneth Clark, *The Other Half: A Self-Portrait* (London, 1977), p.78

72 The main loss in 1917 was the Book Production Gallery and main Reading Room, when both were commandeered to provide office space for the Board of Education. A notice issued by the V&A's Director on 2 October 1917 announced that 'The Library will remain open to holders of Library Tickets until 10pm on Mondays, Thursdays and Saturdays' (V&A Archive: ED84/219).

73 Standing Commission on Museums and Galleries, *The National Museums and Galleries: The War Years and After* (London, 1948)

74 Elizabeth Sears, 'The Warburg Institute 1933–1944: A Precarious Experiment in International Collaboration', *Art Libraries Journal* (2013), vol. 38, no. 4, pp.7–15

75 Wheen (cited note 52), p.48

76 Harthan's many publications include *Bookbindings in the Victoria and Albert Museum* (London, 1950; 3rd edn 1985), and *Books of Hours and their Owners* (London and New York, 1977; 3rd edn 1988).

77 Lightbown's other major books during his time as Keeper of the National Art Library were *Donatello and Michelozzo* (London, 1980) and *Mantegna* (Berkeley, CA, 1986).

78 Anon., 'John Harthan: Obituary', *The Times* (21 February 2003), p.38

79 A.L. Rees and Frances Borzello (eds), *The New Art History* (London, 1986); Peter Vergo (ed.), *The New Museology* (London, 1989). The V&A established its Research Department in 1989, with offices initially in the Library.

80 For the rise of the new heritage professionals, see Julius Bryant (ed.), *Alec Cobbe: Designs for Historic Interiors* (London, 2013), pp.29–30

81 Nigel Reynolds, 'Museums Where Love Is the Main Attraction', *Daily Telegraph* (6 May 2006), p.3

82 The establishment of a dedicated post of Curator of Photographs in 1977 does not imply that the field had been neglected by the V&A. From 1964 Carol Hogben collected the work of twentieth-century photographers, and organized exhibitions for the Circulation Department to send to colleges, as well as at the V&A, such as one on *Henri Cartier-Bresson* in 1969. See Haworth-Booth (cited note 50), pp.141–55

83 Victoria and Albert Museum, *Review of the Years 1974–78* (London, 1981), p.69

84 Bruce Boucher et al., 'The National Art Library', *Burlington Magazine* (1979), vol. 121, p.382

85 Elizabeth Esteve-Coll, 'Image and Reality: The National Art Library', *Art Libraries Journal* (1986), vol. 11, no. 2, pp.33–9

86 Jan van der Wateren, 'The National Art Library: Into the 1990s', *Art Libraries Journal* (1990), vol. 15, no. 4, pp.12–18, describes how he sought 'to imbue our staff with a library-culture rather than a museum-culture'.

87 Lord Armstrong of Ilminster, *The Future of the National Art Library* (London, 1997), unpaginated

88 For a discussion of this issue in other museum libraries, see Andrew Robison, 'Curatorial Reflections on Print Rooms and Libraries', *RBM: A Journal of Rare Books, Manuscripts and Cultural Heritage* (Spring 2007), vol. 8, no. 1, pp.35–44

89 The Keepers of the Department of Engraving, Illustration and Design were Lt.-Col. E.F. Strange (1909–21), Martin Hardie (1921–35), Basil Long (1935–7), James Laver (1938–59), Graham Reynolds (1959–74), Michael Kauffmann (1974–85), John Murdoch (1986–9) and Susan Lambert (1989–2003). EID joined the Department of Paintings under Martin Hardie, and in 1961 was renamed the Department of Paintings and Department of Prints and Drawings. It later became Prints, Drawings and Paintings.

90 *Dickens* was curated by Graham Reynolds and *Byron* by John Murdoch with Anthony Burton.

91 A total of 247 manuscripts, books and periodicals are now on long-term display in the V&A's galleries.

92 *V&A Strategic Plan 2011–2015* (London, 2012), p.3

Rowan Watson: 'The Growth of the Library Collection'

1 Elizabeth Leedham-Green et al. (eds), *Cambridge History of Libraries in Britain and Ireland,* 3 vols (Cambridge, 2006), vol. 2, pp.380–87. A positive assessment of these libraries is given in Martyn Walker, '"For the last many years in England everybody has been educating the people, but they have forgotten to find them any books": The Mechanics' Institutes Library Movement and its Contribution to Working-Class Education during the Nineteenth Century', *Library and Information Studies* (November 2013), vol. 29, no. 4, pp.272–86; the quotation in the title comes from a statement made before the Parliamentary Select Committee on Public Libraries in 1849.

2 *Report from the Select Committee on Arts and their Connexion with Manufacturers,* 4 September 1835, Cmd 598, p.140, Appendix no. 3

3 See the introduction to Dyce's drawing book, *The Drawing Book of the Government School of Design, Published under the Immediate Supervision of the Council,* parts 1 (June 1842) and 2 (August 1842).

4 See Malcolm Baker and Brenda Richardson (eds), *A Grand Design: The Art of the Victoria and Albert Museum* (London and Baltimore, 1997), pp.53, 57, 150. The panels were de-accessioned in the 1960s.

5 The Library's contents are described in the *Third Report of the Council of the School of Design,* for the year 1843–4 (London, 1844), Appendix, pp.54–7

6 The first report of the library, by Ralph Wornum, 'Librarian', after its removal to Marlborough House appeared in Appendix G of the *First Report of the Department of Science and Art* (London, 1854), pp.333–44. The library was called 'the Library of Art', and Wornum reported that some but by no means all 'important deficiencies' had been made good by purchase at the sales of the libraries of A.W.N. Pugin (1812–1852) and Isidore-Justin-Séverin Taylor ('le Baron Taylor', 1789–1879). Public demand, according to Wornum, showed 'a great public necessity for a library of the kind now established in connexion with the Department'.

7 Ralph N. Wornum, *An Account of the Library of the Division of Art at Marlborough House* (London, 1855)

8 The *Catalogue of the Art Library* was published as a proof by the HMSO in 1861 in an edition with the words 'Under review' on the title page; in 1862 came an edition 'for the use of students frequenting the Art Library and for the provincial schools which have the privilege of obtaining books on loan; it is not published for sale'. See Elizabeth James, *The Victoria and Albert Museum: A Bibliography and Exhibition Catalogue 1852–1996* (London and Chicago, 1998), pp.17 (V.1861.001) and 18 (V.1862.001)

9 *Fifteenth Report of the Science and Art Department of the Committee of Council on Education,* Cmd 19661 (London, 1868), p.238. The drawings, PDP 4858–4887 and 4930–4934, costing £71 and £42 respectively, were acquired on 3 July and 24 August 1866; a note in the register comments: 'Part of a set delivered Dec. 1863[?]'; they were received 'From the Secretary's Office', suggesting that they came to the Library through the highest channels. Grüner published the drawings as *The Terracotta Architecture of North Italy,* with texts by Vittore Ottolino and Friedrich Lose, ed. L. Grüner (London, 1867); the book was acquired by the Library in 1867.

10 PDP 1573–1673

11 V&A: P.14–1934 is the preparatory painting by Reuben Townroe

12 N. McWilliam and V. Sekules (eds), *Life and Landscape: P.H. Emerson: Art and Photography in East Anglia 1885–1900* (Norwich, 1986), p.7

13 The rear covers of the exhibition catalogues give instructions how to obtain photographs. For the catalogues, see James (cited note 8), pp.23–6, V.1866.002, V.1867.003, V.1868.002. The art schools had copies of the photographs as of right.

14 Anthony Hamber, *'A Higher Branch of the Art': Photographing the Fine Arts in England 1839–1880* (Amsterdam, 1996)

15 On such collections, see Robert Meyrick, '"Spoils of the Lumber-room": Early Collectors of Wood-Engraved Illustrations from 1860s Periodicals', in Paul Goldman and Simon Cooke (eds), *Reading Victorian Illustration 1855–1875: Spoils of the Lumber Room* (Farnham, 2012), pp.17ff.

16 For the cuttings from illuminated manuscripts, see the *Catalogue of Illuminated Manuscripts: Part II* [Part I never published]: *Miniatures, Leaves and Cuttings* (London, 1908), with attributions provided by Sydney Cockerell; *Catalogue of Miniatures, Leaves and Cuttings from Illuminated Manuscripts* (rev. edn, London, 1923). The cuttings from printed materials have been used in exhibitions but there is no catalogue. The use of cuttings is discussed in Rowan Watson, 'Educators, Collectors, Fragments and the "Illuminations" Collection at the Victoria and Albert Museum in the Nineteenth Century', in Linda L. Brownrigg and Margaret M. Smith (eds), *Interpreting and Collecting Fragments of Medieval Books* (Los Altos Hills, CA, and London, 2000), pp.21–46

17 See the preface by Rowan Watson in Ronald Lightbown and Alan Caiger-Smith (eds and trans.), *The Three Books of the Potter's Art … by … Piccolpasso* (Vendin-le-Vieil, 2007)

18 Paul Williamson, *Medieval Ivory Carvings* (London, 2010), cat. no. 41, pp.168–75; V&A: T.136–1936

19 The name is given as Hippesley, but this may well have been a misprint for Hippisley. Sir John Hippisley Bt (1745/6–1825) had a son named John.

20 Graham Reynolds, *Victoria and Albert Museum: Catalogue of the Constable Collection* (London, 1973), pp.2–6

21 Simon Cooke, *Illustrated Periodicals of the 1860s* (London and Delaware, 2010), p.17

22 See note 8

23 The collection was the subject of a microform publication, *Trade Catalogues in the Victoria and Albert Museum* (London, 1984–6): Conway, Silber & Fleming; Liberty's catalogues 1881–1949: fashion, design, furnishings; industrial and commercial 1785–1937; domestic and household 1762–1939; fashion 1900–33.

24 On the holdings to 1999, see Elizabeth Lomas, *Guide to the Archive of Art and Design* (London, 2001)

25 'The Cestus of Aglaia', in E.T. Cook and Alexander Wedderburn (eds), *The Works of John Ruskin,* 39 vols (London, 1903–12), vol. XIX

26 On autographs, see A.N.L. Munby, *The Cult of the Autograph Letter* (Oxford, 1962). The best overview of Forster's manuscripts remains the catalogue of Richard Forster Sketchley (1826–1911), *Forster Collection: A Catalogue of the Paintings, Manuscripts, Autograph Letters, Pamphlets etc. Bequeathed by John Forster* (London, 1893).

27 Clare Phillips, *Jewels and Jewellery* (London, 2000), pp.18–19

28 See Chapter 2 of *Hard Times,* first published in 1854, discussed in K.J. Fielding, 'Charles Dickens and the Department of Practical Art', *The Modern Language Review* (July 1953), vol. 48, no. 3, pp.270–7. An article by Henry Morley, 'A House Full of Horrors', in the magazine edited by Charles Dickens, *Household Words* (vol. VI, no. 141, 4 December 1852, pp.265–70), poked fun at the 'Correct Principles of Good Taste' displayed by the museum at Marlborough House. See also Philip Collins, *Dickens and Education* (London, 1965), pp.153–9

29 Christopher Wilk (ed.), *Western Furniture: 1350 to the Present Day* (London, 1996), p.12

30 For the three copies of Shakespeare's first folio in the Library (from the Jones, Dyce and Forster collections), see Eric Rasmussen and Anthony James West (eds), *Shakespeare's First Folios* (Basingstoke and New York, 2012), pp.92–103.

31 On the manuscript, see *Art and Design for All: The Victoria and Albert Museum,* ed. Julius Bryant (London, 2011), p.153 no.99.

32 See Charles Sebag-Montefiore, *A Dynasty of Dealers: John Smith and his Successors 1801–1924: A Study of the Art Market in Nineteenth-century London* (London, 2013); the manuscripts are now MSL/1936/2570–2586.

33 MSL/1981/34 (Le Vasseur); MSL/1982/34 (Leach), MSL/1986/10 (Bowman), MSL/1986/1 (Frank Pick)

34 AAD/1982/1 and AAD/1990/4 (House of Worth); AAD/1986/13 (Cecil Beaton); AAD/1991/11 (Gaby Schreiber)

35 Barbara Morris, *Inspiration for Design:*

The Influence of the Victoria and Albert Museum (London, 1986), pp.104, 106

36 Walter Crane, 'A Short Survey of the Art of the Nineteenth Century', *William Morris to Whistler: Papers and Addresses on Art and Craft and the Commonweal* (London, 1911), p.232; Marius Vachon, *La Guerre artistique avec l'Allemagne: l'organisation de la victoire* (Paris, 1916), pp.29, 138–50, 186–204

37 The furore about the display of Art Nouveau furniture given to the Museum in 1900 is described in Christopher Wilk (ed.), *Western Furniture* (London, 1996), pp.11–12. The *Burlington Magazine* (1908–9), vol. XIV, p.132, was aware that the Museum possessed 'decadent and effete examples' (of design and manufacture), but saw no harm in displaying them next to 'healthier' work if labels made the differences clear.

38 On the poster sales, see Howard Coutts and Claire Jones, *Toulouse Lautrec and the Art of the French Poster* (Bowes Museum, County Durham, 2004). *The Studio* magazine's feature on Grasset insisted on the significance of this designer: see Octave Uzanne, 'Eugene Grasset and Decorative Art in France', *The Studio* (1894), vol. 4, no. 20, pp.37–47. *The Studio*, 'an illustrated magazine of fine and applied art', was founded in 1893 to bring international art and design to the attention of an English-speaking readership.

39 See Emma Sutton, *Aubrey Beardsley and British Wagnerism in the 1890s* (Oxford, 2002); Adolphe Jullien, *Richard Wagner: sa vie et ses oeuvres, ouvrage orné de 14 lithographies originales par M. [Henri] Fantin-Latour* (Paris and London, 1880); John Grand-Carteret, *Richard Wagner en caricatures: 130 reproductions … dessins originaux de J. Blas, Moloch et Tiret-Bognet* (Paris, [1891])

40 French editions of 1546 and 1554 were recorded in the catalogue of 1861, but the original edition of 1499 arrived by 1870, with another copy in 1886.

41 For the growth of the manuscript collection, see the introduction in Rowan Watson, *Western Illuminated Manuscripts: A Catalogue of Works in the National Art Library from the Eleventh to the Early Twentieth Century, with a Complete Account of the George Reid Collection*, photography by Paul Gardner, 3 vols (London, 2011); the cuttings are discussed in Watson (cited note 16).

42 *Burlington Magazine* (1904), vol. V, p.513. This editorial referred to the dismissal in 1899 of the head of the V&A Library, James Weale, as evidence of incompetent management; the comment that the Library was 'little known or used' seems strange, given that there were 17,610 visits in 1904 (19,824 in 1905), though the 1890s attendance had averaged 22,000.

43 The brief details of 15 art museum libraries in Joan M. Benedetti (ed.), *Art Museum Libraries and Librarianship* (Maryland and Plymouth, 2007), pp.229–46, show that almost all were chiefly intended for curatorial research, with minimal attendance by the public.

Elizabeth James: 'Collecting the Art and Design of the Book after 1909'

1 The Victoria and Albert Museum Art Division, *Report of the Committee of Re-arrangement* (London, 1908), p.18

2 Case inventories of books exhibited, V&A Archive, MA/38/1/10, MA/38/2

3 *Report of the Committee of Re-arrangement* (cited note 1), pp.19–20: '[T]he Committee would urge that the Victoria and Albert Museum is not, and never can be, a Museum of Commercial Products.' In order to 'improve the artistic quality of British design and production' its collections must either 'illustrate the development of technique or design, or serve as examples of artistic taste', and the judgement of time was needed to ascertain especially the latter point.

4 Cecil H. Smith, *Report for the Years 1909 and 1910 on the Victoria and Albert Museum and the Bethnal Green Museum* (London, 1911), p.13

5 *Review of the Principal Acquisitions* (1911), p.28. This series of illustrated annual reviews was published until 1939.

6 T.J. Cobden-Sanderson, *The Ideal Book or Book Beautiful: A Tract on Calligraphy, Printing, and Illustration and on the Book Beautiful as a Whole* (Hammersmith, 1900), p.1

7 *Report of the Committee of Re-arrangement* (cited note 1), pp.34–5

8 '[S]ince the work of this section is intimately connected with that of the department of Engraving, Illustration and Design, the arrangement of the exhibition shall be carried out after consultation with the officer in charge of that department.' *Report of the Committee of Re-arrangement* (1909), p.35

9 Smith (cited note 4), p.13

10 Cobden-Sanderson (cited note 6), p.6

11 E.F. Strange, *Alphabets: A Manual of Lettering for the Use of Students* (London 1895; 3rd edn 1898) [information from Alan Crawford, 'Johnston, Edward (1872–1944)', in *Oxford Dictionary of National Biography*, online edn: http://www.oxforddnb.com/view/article/34209, accessed 19 December 2013]

12 Published in facsimile by the V&A: Edward Johnston, *The House of David, his Inheritance: A Book of Sample Scripts AD 1914* (London, 1966)

13 MSL/1977/5161; see Rowan Watson, *Western Illuminated Manuscripts: A Catalogue of Works in the National Art Library* (London, 2011), no. 125

14 For example, from the Estonian calligrapher Villu Toots

15 Joyce Irene Whalley and Vera C. Kaden, *The Universal Penman: A Survey of Western Calligraphy from the Roman Period to 1980* (London, 1980)

16 J.I. Whalley, 'The Twentieth Century and the Calligraphic Revival', in *The Art of Calligraphy: Western Europe and America* (London, 1980), pp.329–31

17 Peter Castle (ed.), *Berthold Wolpe: A Retrospective Survey* (London, 1980)

18 Christopher Calderhead, *Illuminating the Word: The Making of the Saint John's Bible* (Collegeville, MN, 2005)

19 Smith (cited note 4), p.55

20 S.T. Prideaux, *Notes on Printing and Bookbinding: A Guide to the Exhibition of Tools and Materials Used in the Processes* (London, 1921)

21 *V&A Museum Circulation Department: Its History and Scope* [1950?]

22 Correspondence concerning the French commissions, 1949–51, held in the V&A Archive, VAL49/175. Wheen and Floud were perhaps inspired by the Arts Council exhibition of Major Abbey's modern bindings, for which Abbey had commissioned no fewer than 14 new pieces. 'He is probably the only English bibliophile to possess a group of contemporary French bindings … The Arts Council is deeply grateful to him for the opportunity of showing this selection from his modern bindings and thus calling attention to the need for a revival of this forgotten craft, which has so long and honourable a history'; catalogue by Philip James, *An Exhibition of Modern English and French Bindings from the Collection of Major J.R. Abbey* (London, 1949).

23 Letter from General Manager, Zaehnsdorf Ltd, to The Librarian, 15 May 1952. V&A Archive MA/37/6/6

24 The Department also supports the Designer Bookbinders, and the Society of Scribes and Illuminators, as the repository for their archives.

25 R.C. Kenedy acknowledged the support and influence of Designer Bookbinders in helping to envisage the scope of his exhibition *The Open and Closed Book* in 1979: *The Open and Closed Book: Contemporary Book Arts* (London, 1979), p. [vii]

26 Ibid.

27 John Harthan, introduction in Ivor Robinson and Bernard Middleton (eds), *Modern British Bookbindings: An Exhibition of Modern British Bookbinding by Members of Designer Bookbinders* (London, 1971), p.7

28 R.C. Kenedy, in *The Open and Closed Book* (cited note 25), p.37

29 Monroe K. Wheeler, *Modern Painters and Sculptors as Illustrators* (New York, 1936)

30 Carol Hogben and Rowan Watson, *From Manet to Hockney: Modern Artists' Illustrated Books* (London, 1985), p.262. Mourlot's firm were the leading art lithographers. The letterpress was printed by the Fanfare Press (for whom Laver wrote an introduction for a collection of ornaments designed by Berthold Wolpe).

31 'Book Illustrations by Matisse, Picasso and Rouault', exhibition press release, V&A Archive MA/51/1/1

32 Tessa Sidey, *Editions Alecto: Original Graphics, Multiple Originals 1960–1981* (Aldershot, 2003)

33 Cathy Courtney (ed.), *Speaking of Book Art: Interviews with British and American Book Artists* (Los Altos Hills, CA, and London, 1999), p.10

34 Ibid., p.27

35 Peter Floud, memorandum to Arthur Wheen, 1 February 1950, V&A Archive, MA/37/6/6. The book was acquired in 1946.

36 Hogben and Watson (cited note 30). Included from the earlier period were *Le Morte Darthur* with Beardsley's illustrations, the Kelmscott Chaucer and the first book of Lucien Pissarro's Eragny Press.

37 Today The Enid Linder Foundation is the financial supporter of the V&A Illustration Awards.

38 The term 'photo book', which does not appear (2013) in the *Oxford English Dictionary*, apparently became current between 2001 (Andrew Roth, ed., *The Book of 101 Books: Seminal Photographic Books of the Twentieth Century*, New York, 2001) and 2004

(Martin Parr and Gerry Badger, *The Photobook: A History*, vol. 1, London, 2004).

39 Exceptions notwithstanding, including the Vale Press (Charles Ricketts), Eragny Press (Lucien Pissarro), Circle Press (Ronald King – see above, p.52), Ken Campbell.

40 *Exhibition of Works by the Italian Futurist Painters*, March 1912 (London, 1912)

41 Jeremy Aynsley, 'Modern Commercial Typography, 1936: An Archive of Jobbing Printing at the Victoria and Albert Museum', *Journal of the Decorative Arts Society* (1995), no. 19, pp.59–66

42 A display from the collection, 'Artists' Graphic Design before World War II', was presented in 1985 as an 'offshoot' of *From Manet to Hockney*.

43 'a throwaway . . . "Elijah is coming"', James Joyce, *Ulysses* [1922] (New York, 1984), episode 10, line 294

44 'Introduction', in *The International Surrealist Exhibition* [catalogue] (1936), p.13

45 'Contents', in *The Open and Closed Book* (cited note 25), p. [v]

46 Malcolm Quantrill, 'Robert Kenedy, 1926–1980', *Art International* (1981), vol. 25, pp.156–9

47 *Art in America* (1980), vol. 68, p.194

48 Kenedy acknowledges their 'collaboration' in *The Open and Closed Book* (cited note 25), p.8

49 Kenedy considered that 'No significant signs of modernity are evident in contemporary trends of printing with *movable* type' but as yet 'no national museum in the world appears to have honoured this new craft [fount design for photosetting] with a[n] . . . exhibition of its achievement', *The Open and Closed Book* (cited note 25), p.57

50 '[A]s so convincingly demonstrated by John Sparrow', ibid., p.49; ref. John Sparrow, *Visible Words: A Study of Inscriptions in and as Books and Works of Art* (Cambridge, 1969) [originated in the author's Sandars lectures, an annual series at Cambridge]

51 R.C. Kenedy, 'Ian Hamilton Finlay', *Art International* (1973), vol. 17, no. iii, pp.37–9. Kenedy also curated *Two Contemporary Presses: Wild Hawthorn Press, Journeyman Press*, a display in the Library Gallery at the V&A, 1974.

52 *The Open and Closed Book* (cited note 25), p. [viii]

53 Ibid., p.99

54 By Michael Chave, of Face Type Ltd. (The V&A's current fount family was designed by Wolf Olins as part of a complete rebranding in 2002.)

55 Eugen Gomringer (1954), quoted in Mary Ellen Solt (ed.), *Hispanic Arts* (Richmond, VA, 1968), vol. 1 no. 3–4, p.67

56 It was a mannerism of the period, consistently observed by houédard, to refrain from upper case, especially in one's own name, symbolizing an egalitarian ethos.

57 Guy Brett and Hugh Wakefield, *Dsh, Dom sylvester houédard, Visual Poetries: A Victoria and Albert Museum Loan Exhibition* (London, [1971?])

58 Thomas A. Clark, *Moschatel: Comments by the Publisher* [one sheet] (Nailsworth, [1980s?])

59 'Moschatel Press', *Umbrella* (1984), vol. 7, no. 1, p.27

60 The relationship with Coracle was reinforced in 2008 when the V&A showed an exhibition curated by Simon Cutts on a group of artist-poet small presses: *Certain Trees: The Constructed Book, Poem and Object 1964–2006* (Saint-Yrieix-la-Perche, 2006)

61 For example, Clive Phillpot, 'Twentysix Gasoline Stations That Shook the World: The Rise and Fall of Cheap Booklets as Art', *Art Libraries Journal* (1993), vol. 18, pp.4–13

62 Also in the Conceptual chapter Kenedy included (non-photographic) books by the important early American Conceptualists Sol LeWitt and Lawrence Weiner, with the justification that they had been published in London.

63 The term was probably first coined in America, but by 1976 the Arts Council had assembled a touring exhibition: Martin Attwood and Clive Philpot, *Artists' Books: Booklets, Pamphlets, Catalogues, Periodicals, Anthologies and Magazines Almost All Published since 1970* (London, 1976)

64 For example, Dieter Roth published by Hansjörg Mayer classed with 'Private press books'

65 Twenty-three definitions were assembled by Simon Ford in 'Artists' Books in UK and Eire Libraries', unpublished MA dissertation, University of Northumbria, 1992, pp.77–81

66 The first discussion in book form took place in 1985: Joan Lyons (ed.), *Artists' Books: A Critical Anthology and Sourcebook* (Rochester, NY, 1985), as well as the entry into the field of Anne Moeglin Delcroix, a central commentator, with an exhibition at the Centre Pompidou in Paris: *Livres d'artistes*, in which she rehearsed the classification of types later developed in her *Esthétique du livre d'artiste 1960/1980* (Paris, 1997; 2nd edn 2012).

67 Van der Wateren was preceded for two years by Elizabeth Estève-Coll, who then became Director of the Museum. She too had experience and knowledge of artist publishing and encouraged acquisitions from the Circle Press, among others.

68 Acquired from the curator and collector Elias Redstone

69 *Review of the Principal Acquisitions* (1911), p.28

70 In 1978, notwithstanding 'the constant rise in the price of books', the Library claimed 'comprehensive coverage of the fine, decorative and applied arts of all ages and countries' (*Review of the Years 1974–1978*, London, 1981, p.65). Recent collecting policies contain a much fuller and more nuanced picture of the decision-making framework, necessarily at considerable length: 'National Art Library Policy for the Development of Documentary Materials', *V&A Collections Development Policy* (2010), Appendix 6.0, pp.106–17: http://www.vam.ac.uk/__data/assets/pdf_file/0009/176967/v-and-a-collections-development-policy.pdf [accessed 29 October 2013]

71 '[T]hree copies of "Arms and Armour at Sandringham" were presented by command of Her Majesty Queen Alexandra in accordance with the intention of His late Majesty King Edward VII . . . From Mr Pierpont Morgan was received a copy of the catalogue of his collection of jewels and precious works of art . . . sumptuously produced on Japanese vellum with wonderful hand-coloured facsimiles, in an edition of 40 copies only, for private circulation'. Smith (cited note 4), p.58

72 *The Art Periodicals Collection at the V&A Museum, 1750–1920* (London, 1986–94). This microform set comprises: 1. Ackermann's *Repository of art* and other titles – 2. *The artist, L'art, Courrier de l'art* and other titles – *Art and decoration – Christian art.*

73 Douglas Dodds and Aileen Cook, 'The National Art Library, ARLIS/UK & Ireland and the Union List of Art, Architecture and Design Serials', *Serials Librarian* (1997), vol. 32, nos 3–4, pp.127–37

74 Trevor Fawcett and Clive Phillpot (eds), *The Art Press: Two Centuries of Art Magazines: Essays Published on the Occasion of the International Conference on Art Periodicals and the Exhibition* The Art Press *at the Victoria and Albert Museum, London* (London, 1976). Includes essays by Anthony Burton (who curated the exhibition), Hans Brill, Jane Beckett, John A. Walker and the editors. The exhibition itself was also published on microfiche: *The Art Press: Two Centuries of the Art Periodical: An Exhibition Held at the Victoria and Albert Museum* (Cambridge, 1977), with 24 microfiches showing the exhibits.

75 Simon Ford, 'Contemporary Art and Publishing', in James Bettley (ed.), *The Art of the Book: From Medieval Manuscript to Graphic Novel* (London, 2001), pp.186–205

76 In the 1980s, too, a short series of conferences on 'Art and Communication' was organized in collaboration with the Wimbledon School of Art; see, for example, *Art Publishing and Art Publics Today: Transcript of a . . . Conference Held in . . . the Victoria and Albert Museum* (London, 1989).

77 http://www.vam.ac.uk/vastatic/wid/exhibits/bookandbeyond/ [accessed 1 December 2013]. Douglas Dodds, *The Book and Beyond: Electronic Publishing and the Art of the Book* (London, 1995)

78 By analogy, a category of 'Audio-visual aids' was included in *The Open and Closed Book* (cited note 25): on show were examples of educational resources alongside cartoon films and slide-animated concrete poetry. Ibid., p.123

79 See also *The Agrippa Files*: http://agrippa.english.ucsb.edu/ [accessed 3 December 2013]

80 *The V&A's Computer Art Collections*: http://www.vam.ac.uk/content/articles/t/v-and-a-computer-art-collections/ [accessed 3 December 2013]

Index

Concordance

Picture Credits